M000190482

²¹ "The son said to him, 'Fat
against you. I am no longer wor

²² "But the father said to his
and put it on him. Put a ring on his finger and sandals on his feet. ²³ Bring the fattened calf and kill it. Let's have a feast and celebrate. ²⁴ For this son of mine was dead and is alive again; he was lost and is found.' So they began to celebrate.

²⁵ "Meanwhile, the older son was in the field. When he came near the house, he heard music and dancing. ²⁶ So he called one of the servants and asked him what was going on. ²⁷ 'Your brother has come,' he replied, 'and your father has killed the fattened calf because he has him back safe and sound.'

²⁸ "The older brother became angry and refused to go in. So his father went out and pleaded with him. ²⁹ But he answered his father, 'Look! All these years I've been slaving for you and never disobeyed your orders. Yet you never gave me even a young goat so I could celebrate with my friends. ³⁰ But when this son of yours who has squandered your property with prostitutes comes home, you kill the fattened calf for him!'

³¹ "'My son,' the father said, 'you are always with me, and everything I have is yours. ³² But we had to celebrate and be glad, because this brother of yours was dead and is alive again; he was lost and is found.'"

17. Scripture taken from the HOLY BIBLE NEW INTERNATIONAL VERSION (Grand Rapids, Zondervan Copyright 1973, 1978, 1984)

Luke 10: The Good Samaritan

Just then a religion scholar stood up with a question to test Jesus. "Teacher, what do I need to do to get eternal life?"

²⁶ He answered, "What's written in God's Law? How do you interpret it?"

²⁷ He said, "That you love the Lord your God with all your passion and prayer and muscle and intelligence—and that you love your neighbor as well as you do yourself."

²⁸ "Good answer!" said Jesus. "Do it and you'll live."

[29] Looking for a loophole, he asked, "And just how would you define 'neighbor'?"

[30-32] Jesus answered by telling a story. "There was once a man traveling from Jerusalem to Jericho. On the way he was attacked by robbers. They took his clothes, beat him up, and went off leaving him half-dead. Luckily, a priest was on his way down the same road, but when he saw him he angled across to the other side. Then a Levite religious man showed up; he also avoided the injured man.

[33-35] "A Samaritan traveling the road came on him. When he saw the man's condition, his heart went out to him. He gave him first aid, disinfecting and bandaging his wounds. Then he lifted him onto his donkey, led him to an inn, and made him comfortable. In the morning he took out two silver coins and gave them to the innkeeper, saying, 'Take good care of him. If it costs any more, put it on my bill—I'll pay you on my way back.'

[36] "What do you think? Which of the three became a neighbor to the man attacked by robbers?"

[37] "The one who treated him kindly," the religion scholar responded. Jesus said, "Go and do the same."

18. Truth and Reconciliation Canada. (2015). Honouring the truth, reconciling for the future: Summary of the final report of the Truth and Reconciliation Commission of Canada. Winnipeg: Truth and Reconciliation Commission of Canada.

19. Eugene H. Peterson, *The Message: The Bible in Contemporary Language.* (Colorado Springs: NavPress, 2002) Gospel of John, Chapter 13.

Jesus knew that the Father had put him in complete charge of everything, that he came from God and was on his way back to God. So he got up from the supper table, set aside his robe, and put on an apron. Then he poured water into a basin and began to wash the feet of the disciples, drying them with his apron.

20. Scripture taken from the HOLY BIBLE NEW INTERNATIONAL VERSION (Grand Rapids, Zondervan Copyright 1973, 1978, 1984) Matthew 20: 20-28.

Then the mother of Zebedee's sons came to Jesus with her sons and, kneeling down, asked a favor of him.

[21] "What is it you want?" he asked.

She said, "Grant that one of these two sons of mine may sit at your right and the other at your left in your kingdom."

[22] "You don't know what you are asking," Jesus said to them. "Can you drink the cup I am going to drink?"

"We can," they answered.

[23] Jesus said to them, "You will indeed drink from my cup, but to sit at my right or left is not for me to grant. These places belong to those for whom they have been prepared by my Father."

[24] When the ten heard about this, they were indignant with the two brothers. [25] Jesus called them together and said, "You know that the rulers of the Gentiles lord it over them, and their high officials exercise authority over them. [26] Not so with you. Instead, whoever wants to become great among you must be your servant, [27] and whoever wants to be first must be your slave—[28] just as the Son of Man did not come to be served, but to serve, and to give his life as a ransom for many."

21. air07. Justice, Mercy and Grace. Thetruthspeakproject.wordpress.com. August 19, 2011

22. Denny Bellesi and Leesa Bellesi, *The Kingdom Assignment – What will you do with the talents God has given you?* (Grand Rapids: Zondervan, 2001)

23. Scripture taken from the HOLY BIBLE NEW INTERNATIONAL VERSION (Grand Rapids, Zondervan Copyright 1973, 1978, 1984) Romans 5: 1-5 Therefore, since we have been justified through faith, we[a] have peace with God through our Lord Jesus Christ, [2] through whom we have gained access by faith into this grace in which we now

stand. And we[b] boast in the hope of the glory of God. [3] Not only so, but we[c] also glory in our sufferings, because we know that suffering produces perseverance; [4] perseverance, character; and character, hope. [5] And hope does not put us to shame, because God's love has been poured out into our hearts through the Holy Spirit, who has been given to us.

24. Leah Denbok. *Nowhere to Call Home. Photographs and Stories of the Homeless. Volume One* (Victoria, FriesenPress) 2017.

CPSIA information can be obtained
at www.ICGtesting.com
Printed in the USA
LVHW020917300321
682892LV00030B/2185

IT'S **BUSINESS**, NOT **SOCIAL**™

STANDOUT

Develop and Increase your *Significance* over *Time* with *Authenticity*, *Networking*, *Dedication*, *Open-mindedness*, *Understanding*, and *Tenacity*

COLLEEN McKENNA

DEDICATION

For my husband Geoff and daughters Sydney, Meredith, and Liza.
Thank you for your grace and love all these years. You are the
pleasure of my life.

CONTENTS

ACKNOWLEDGMENTS

Everything at Intero Advisory is a team effort; this book is
no exception.

I have the privilege of working alongside people committed to
sharing their knowledge and expertise with the world. Each member
of our team challenges me to up my game, think differently, be bold.
This book is a testament to their encouragement and belief that we
have something special at Intero and everyone can benefit from
what we know.

I love words. I love how they look on a page, how they sound and
how they inspire, inform, and encourage others. I learned long ago
not to fall in love with my own words. I couldn't. I've turned my
words over to people I trust. I've come to rely on editors to ensure
that I communicate clearly and with conviction. Basically, they
save me from myself on a weekly basis. I've relied on the editorial
talents of Yvonne Lyons, Erin Dore Miller, Sarah Bentley, and
Charlotte Zang.

They told me when I could riff, reined me in when I flew off course,
and reminded me that every word needs to count for something.
Thanks to each of you. I'm still not grammar-literate. However, I'm
closer than I've ever been.

Shouts, kudos, and thanks to Sydney Cusick, Liza Slavin, Jim
Cusick, Meredith Cusick, Iliana Sanza, Matt Culloty, Sarah Bentley,
Charlotte Zang, Jody Walstrom, and Marney Lumpkin. They are the
team that makes everything at Intero happen.

They feed me the questions, feedback, and comments clients share.
Much of what they share makes its way to our blogs and into this
book. The Intero team brings our best practices and process to life
for our clients.

Sydney, Meredith, and Liza are my daughters AND colleagues. Through the years, the joys and the valleys, you have been my rock. I am proud beyond words.

Jim is my son-in-law and is always thinking and building greatness into all we do. You are the micro-improvement aficionado. Thank you for being part of our team and family.

Sarah, I am so grateful you're back. You always have a smile and give me a nod even when I know you're wondering, "What did she just say? What do I need to do?" You make it look easy.

Matt, fellow Spring Laker, so glad Meredith found your name on Rick Byrd's website and I emailed you. You are the ideal web developer and designer for us. Your work is a testament to the firepower of your left and right brain working together.

Charlotte Zang, thank you for your guidance, commitment, and get-it-done attitude. From the hundreds of LinkedIn profiles you write every year to this book, you have been part of our team for years. From the first time we met in 2005, you've been a trusted partner and friend.

There are people who along their career journey stopped at Intero and left an indelible stamp on who we are. Each of them contributed at a high level and while a part of our team were integral to our success and served as loyal ambassadors of our small and mighty business. They include Lindsey McMillion Stemann, Alicia Dodd, Lynne Leidy, Charlotte Meredith, and Erin Dore Miller.

Many others have contributed and include our centers of influence or community of influencers. To those featured in this book, again, I thank you.

A big shoutout to Ben Griffin, Ellen Moore, Ed Mullin, Scott Carpenter, Denise O'Neill, Eliott Wagonheim, Lynda Katz Wilner, and Larry Wilner for your friendship over the years. There are dozens, no, hundreds of you. If we talked or you've mentioned us to a friend or colleague, thank you!

Thank you to the Vistage community of Chairs, Speakers, and members. You have taught me so much about leadership and working through issues with clarity and insight. Shaun Bradley, Arturo Lopez, Mark Murphy, Stephen Tafaro, Chris Quinn, Jim Blomberg, Julie Heisey, Kevin McKeown, and Anna Kennedy, you are among the finest leaders I know. As clients, each of you has made us better. Thank you.

To Dean Minuto, thank you for contributing to this effort. Yes, you were among the first to say, "You must have a book. It's there. Get going." Every conversation with you is rich with story and learning woven together with wit and salty language for some down-home shock value.

To Des McCabe, I am delighted that you were so easy to find on Google. You are as real as they get. Your warmth and expertise carried us through the process of a whole new business model with ease and excitement. You are the ultimate consultant and let us find the answers to create something powerful for those who want to grow their business.

To my ultimate decades-long dear friend and mentor, Claudia Meyers. You have always been an advocate, truth-teller, and generous giver. I remember the first time we met. It was April 9, 1986, my first day of work at *The Baltimore Sun*. You walked right up to my desk, shook my hand and said hello with the biggest smile ever. Through the years we've shared a lifetime of experiences and ups and downs. You have taught me so much and most importantly, you've given me insight no one else would.

To my sister and best friend, Margaret, and my brothers, Alan and Paul, thank you. I'm quite sure I've bored you to tears over the years about this thing called LinkedIn but you listened, nodded, and provided lots of encouragement. Thanks for taking care of me all these years.

And finally, to my soulmate, husband, and life partner Geoff. I cannot imagine that I would have ever found the courage and confidence to pursue life so boldly if it wasn't for you. You have blessed and enriched our lives with your selflessness, love, and ever-present humor. You make me laugh every day. You are the embodiment of all that is good in the world.

FOREWORD

"Colleen, I hate LinkedIn. It actually *hurts* me to log in."

There we were, about to go onstage in New York to be filmed delivering our own Talks in front of an audience of 50 or so CEOs—and I had turned to one of the other expert presenters and told her my truth: "I hate social media. It turns me off. And if I am honest, it scares me."

Because I knew I could do better. And I did not know where to start.

And because that person was Colleen McKenna—and her superpowers are kindness and execution—she smiled that C-Mack smile and said, *"Dino, I will help you with that."*

And she did—in the weeks and months ahead she showed me a path to follow and walked along with me until I learned what to do and how to do it within LinkedIn. Colleen outlines that path for you and your Team in this book.

Two things I can tell you with absolute certainty after more than thirty years of professional study of influence and persuasion: thing one is that humans generally *don't do things* that cause them pain unless there is a *really big gain* involved; and thing two is we *really like people* who (metaphorically speaking) can *connect with us*, put their arm around us and assure us: *"You're not alone, I got your back."*

There is big gain involved for you and your Team in connecting with people by utilizing LinkedIn—especially in times of disruption.

As you read, pay particular attention to Colleen's suggestions regarding "Centers of Influence" (not all your connections are created equal) and "1st Level Connections." Right now, are you even connected with all your best clients?

I am excited for you, because as you execute on Colleen's practical tips and strategies, you and your Team will make more of a difference in the world.

And that is why you do what you do. No matter what your Business is, it is also Personal— and success in life is about making a difference.

With your success in mind,

Dean Minuto
October 1, 2020
St. Pete Beach, Florida
Vistage CEO Speaker of the Year 2015 for the course
YESCALATE® GET TO YES FASTER®

INTRODUCTION

Your time and attention are valuable. I recognize their worth and appreciate that you have many choices as to where to spend your time. Thank you for joining me.

I'm writing this introduction heading into the latter part of 2020.

So much is up in the air at this moment in history.

The books you may have planned to read now feel dated. Other books on distributed teams, WFH (working from home), diversity and inclusion are rushing to publication. It's a brave new world.

Why this book now? Don't take this the wrong way. I think you're ready now.

When LinkedIn launched in 2004, they had a big plan and vision for connecting the world's professionals. Their vision from the beginning has centered around economic opportunity. Their vision is:

> *"To create economic opportunity for every member of the global workforce."*

What an aspirational vision. There is no doubt they are on their way. Will they ever be done? Of course not.

I see new ways of working in the days, years, and decades ahead. How we work needs to work alongside all the roles we shoulder and embrace.

Have people across the globe benefitted from LinkedIn? I believe the answer is yes.

You can now more easily find and apply for a job down the street, across town, in another state, or on another continent.

You can now more easily find and send a message to a CEO, leader, author, speaker, director, manager, recruiter, or anyone else that you might want to connect with in minutes.

You now have the power to push past traditional boundaries and showcase your talent, strengths, experiences, perspective, and vision to others who could benefit from knowing you.

You have the opportunity to advance your career and business initiatives by bringing your real self to the world's largest professional network.

You, CEO, emerging professional, and everyone in your organization are the face of your company by positioning yourself as an ambassador. This is how careers and business initiatives are advanced.

It's about you. Everything on these pages is about what you can do to best position yourself to create the future that aligns with your values and beliefs. **Opportunity presents itself when you take action.**

I believe that when you authentically develop your influence through your personal brand and network, you elevate your business and further your career. This is true for you, the CEO, or you, the emerging professional. You may have different resources, opportunities, and levels of experience. However, the playing field is different now and everyone needs to prepare for a time such as this.

Isn't it time you claimed your economic opportunity?

If you've gained competitive advantage, how will you keep it?

This book is about opportunity. Your **opportunity** to propel your career and business forward by managing what is in your control.

I am reluctant to add too many statistics to this book as it often dates the book and the overarching message. However, I do think it's important to benchmark where we are as it relates to employment.

In early October of 2020, the *Wall Street Journal* published several key stats from the September jobs report worth noting. These figures were provided by the U.S. Labor Department and it was the last report before the 2020 presidential election.

- Employers added 661,000 jobs in September.
- The U.S. has replaced 11.4 million of the 22 million jobs lost in March and April at the beginning of the pandemic.
- September's job report marked the first time since April that net hiring was below one million.
- In the Opinion section, the *Wall Street Journal* reports that the U.S. **private** economy added 877,000 new jobs and the government shed 216,000 jobs including 34,000 temporary Census workers.
- The National Federation of Independent Business said in early October that 36% of small businesses had job openings they couldn't fill.
- 60% of construction firms reported few or no qualified applicants and 30% cited a shortage of qualified labor as their top problem.
- Recently Disney, United Airlines, American Airlines and Allstate announced combined layoffs of 68,000 employees.

Companies are hiring and companies are laying off. As usual, both are true.

Applying what you read on these pages is more important than you may realize. Everyone must enhance, dust off, or energize their personal brand and community of connections to ensure your marketability.

As employers bring back, add on, or reconfigure their workforces, they should consider how candidates and current employees manage their personal brands and networks. Hire and retain for a 2021 and beyond economic landscape not a 2000 or worse, a 20th century mindset.

It's Business, Not Social™ will prompt you to think differently, ask new questions, and reduce your learning curve. You need to think differently.

You don't have to like it. More on that later. I do, however, expect you to see the challenge and opportunity in front of you and recommend that you ask yourself, "How will I embrace my professional future?" You and your organization depend on it.

Maybe you need a fresh perspective, encouragement, a nudge, or a roadmap. Regardless, take what you need and get moving.

It's Business, Not Social™ is straightforward and gives you best practices so that you show up more professionally, ready to engage and further your career.

This book is NOT about social media, digital transformation, automation, or selling. I won't espouse rhetoric or theory or promise crazy outcomes.

This book is about building you up professionally in the only way that matters.
You being you.
You being real.
You bringing your best to the world.

If you're reading this and you're the company Champion, you'll need to create the vision of "why" not just "how" and share that with everyone in your organization. Especially leadership.

Throughout these pages, we'll focus on telling your story, nurturing and expanding the people who are your influencers, evangelists, and raving fans so that your career and business opportunities thrive.

I will focus everything on our **It's Business, Not Social™ method** for building a personal brand and a community of influence and influencers to further your career and business. I think it's more than that, though.

The days ahead will be radically different than they were in early 2020. Those days are so far behind us. It's why we're amping up our vision and thinking bigger than ever before.

While we're known for our LinkedIn expertise, we do so much more than maximize LinkedIn. **We advance our clients' career and business initiatives.** This is why we're stepping out and expanding our business with certified **Licensed Partners** who will enhance their business using our training and coaching content.

Our **Licensed Partners** will further our collective vision so that people and companies across the globe can position themselves to stand out and create new career and business opportunities.

Each of us is responsible for our careers and businesses — the highs and lows. We need to be comfortable with being seen and known. We know how to impart the insight others need to accomplish this effectively.

Defining My Future

In the fourth quarter of 2010, I knew I would lose my job as head of sales for a printing company that had been highly regarded but had fallen out of favor for several reasons. The recession and digital world contributed to the company's decline, no doubt. More significant than those two forces was an impenetrable lack of vision and open-mindedness from members of leadership.

After a recession, I saw being fired for the first time at age 50 as a rite of passage in an uncertain world. However, I couldn't see myself working in another toxic environment, and if I were going to fail, it would be on my terms.

While most people begin businesses because they have deep expertise in a skill or topic, I realized that I didn't have that. I did not want to be a sales trainer. Reviewing my three-ring binder of personality and work assessments, I realized my strengths were building relationships, creating a vision, and providing a method that is built for long-term success.

I interviewed more than 50 consultants over 30 days. I wanted to know what they deemed the hardest thing about running their business. Each person shared that it was business development. Aha! That's all I knew how to do. I had to reverse-engineer my business and gain expertise quickly.

Intero Advisory launched in January of 2011 with less than $10,000, a nugget of an idea, and enthusiastic reassurance from my husband and three daughters that I could figure this out and create a sustainable business.

While I was heading down one particular path, people asked me to explain how LinkedIn worked and how to use it. In 2011, LinkedIn was hitting its tipping point and I had already been a member, logging on every day for the last five years. I saw the vision for LinkedIn and knew it would be a game changer for the world's professionals.

I found my niche.

Today, my three daughters, my son-in-law, and yes, my go-to advisor and number one supporter, my husband, and other super talented and valued members of our team from Minnesota to the Eastern Shore of Maryland make up Intero Advisory. I also consider every person a blessing who, along their career path, called Intero Advisory home. Their contributions made us better throughout the years.

We have proven that personalizing your brand and establishing, nurturing, and expanding your network increases your career, new business, and recruiting opportunities. We've guided tens of thousands of professionals and several hundred companies.

Today, those who have worked with us or followed our blog have a better understanding of moving beyond the status quo and building their brand beyond the corporate message and leadership team.

We've guided and supported people through job searches, prospecting, deepening their connection to current clients, attracting talent, and finally, extending their reputation and expertise to a global audience.

I believe everyone across your organization needs to know how to do this well. It's part of a 21st century business mindset and skill set. And it's not about being on social media. It's about being in close proximity with others who value knowing you for your talents, skills, expertise, and of course, authenticity. It's about being social in a way that builds bridges, creates collaboration, and leverages, not limits, people throughout their careers.

To say you don't need to know and engage is another way of expressing or saying:

- You and your role are not significant
- You don't care or are indifferent to developing your best self
- You are above needing to do that because you are so significant

This mindset or attitude is limiting. Careers and businesses don't thrive with limitations set upon them.

Throughout this book, I will introduce you to people, clients mostly, who have elevated their presence, made a commitment to knowing others, and sustained their efforts with positive gain.

It's time to place yourself where you want to be. There are a number of factors that play a part in that happening, some external, but you need to be your own catalyst. Build connections with people you don't know and encourage others to get to know you. Be transparent and open-minded.

Be a STANDOUT

As I reflect on how we help others advance their career and business initiatives and consider our clients who have propelled their personal brands, businesses, and careers, I see that they all have something in common: they **STAND OUT**. They have embraced being a **STANDOUT**.

To me and my team, a **STANDOUT** signifies someone who views their career and business initiatives with a long-term commitment and view. Our definition of **STANDOUT**: **S**ignificance over **T**ime with **A**uthenticity, **N**etworking, **D**edication, **O**pen-mindedness, **U**nderstanding, and **T**enacity. This should be everyone's number one career priority.

Becoming a **STANDOUT** is hard. It's deliberate and it takes time to accomplish. It's lasting though and that's different from building a social media persona. Creating long-term influence and significance is the foundation throughout this book.

Most people don't show up on day one as the CEO. Of course, it may be easier today than ever to start a business and declare yourself the CEO, but that's not what I am referring to. Becoming a CEO of a business that employs others, generates revenue, and is built to last is usually the result of experience, industry or business expertise, and a well-built network of mentors, advisors, and peers.

When I think of my own career, I think of people. Of course, I recall the jobs, the companies, and the responsibilities I held. However, it's the people and the relationships that stand out the most.

No one launches or develops their career without people.

The chapters ahead will dive deeper into these attributes and their importance.

You may agree or disagree as you progress from chapter to chapter. However, I challenge you to reflect on the framework and apply it holistically. And apply you must. I submit that while someone else may handle it for you, managing and expanding your reputation and brand needs collaboration with you.

The sooner you apply our concepts and best practices, the faster you'll have the opportunity to connect, reconnect, and engage with a more significant number of people and gain traction.

CHAPTER 1

You Don't Have to Like It

STANDOUT

Seek opportunity with an open mind and curious nature.

I know very few CEOs, business owners, leaders, or experienced professionals who like social media. I get that. It's partially why from Intero's early days, I differentiated us by continually reminding people that we are not a social media agency and that LinkedIn is not Facebook for adults or anything even remotely like it.

Call me a purist. That's okay. And, yes, a case can be made that LinkedIn is more like Facebook all the time. I encourage our clients to block that out, swipe on past those silly posts and remember why they are there.

LinkedIn is by far the most informative business tool I've leveraged in my decades-long sales career.

Why?

First, it's user-generated or as close to user-generated as you can get.

Second, people who use LinkedIn are there for a common purpose.

Third, you can glean gobs of important information about your peers, potential talent, worthy rivals, professional organizations, and alumni all in one place as quickly as your fingers will type.

So, when you tell me you don't like social media, you will likely see me nod my head and agree with you. However, I'm not talking about social media.

And when you tell me that you don't like LinkedIn because it's all salespeople trying to pitch you things you think you don't need, or that it's not intuitive and it's not valuable because over the years you've connected with so many people you don't know, I will also nod again.

But it's an inevitable part of doing business.

You do it because it's part of your job.

If you hope to position yourself as a leader, an industry-leading company, or a sought-after job candidate, you want to hire the best talent or work with the best clients, you need to take your personal brand and LinkedIn seriously.

You need to be known and you need to set an example for those you lead.

Many of the clients we've worked with over the years realize that the reason they didn't like LinkedIn was because they didn't take the time to understand it. But when someone sat with them and explained its nuances and power, their perspective and attitude changed.

The least informed are often the first to throw something under the bus. My team and I see this over and over and it's why we love coaching and training. It gives us an opportunity to demonstrate the power and depth of LinkedIn's platform.

More than anything, we want CEOs and leaders to know about LinkedIn so that they can ask their teams the right questions.

Consider how you show up

Are you assessing how you show up to others?

Are you presenting yourself in a way that attracts others?

Are you familiar with how LinkedIn and Google work on your behalf?

Are you interested in the success of others?

Your goal should be to control the narrative and showcase who you are.

Ask your team better questions

Rather than ask, "Do you use LinkedIn?" ask your team the following questions:

- "How are you building your personal brand on LinkedIn?"
- "Are you connecting with customers, prospects, influencers, industry leaders?"
- "How are you engaging with those people?"
- "Have you set up any calls or meetings (Zoom included) with those people?"
- "Have you put a messaging sequence in place?"
- "Are you sharing our company's content?"

- "Have you closed any new business?"
- "Have you expanded business as a result of connecting to new people in your customer accounts?"
- "Are you asking for introductions?"
- "What's your connection acceptance rate?"
- "How many people express an interest in talking with you?"
- "Have you recommended any clients lately?"
- "Are you downloading your 1st level connections and looking for new opportunities and unintended gaps?"

Those questions and the answers that follow will provide enormous insight and conversation. They are open-ended questions that will spark next steps and also let others know you are well informed and understand how LinkedIn works best.

That's a win-win.

There are ways to manage LinkedIn so it works on your behalf. I'm not suggesting you respond every time you receive a connection request or notification of a mention. I am suggesting that you carve out time to know how to use LinkedIn, ensure that your sales, marketing, and recruiting teams are highly proficient, and that you're building a strong network of C-level peers.

Save the liking for other things.

If you appreciate what it can do for you and your company, that's good enough.

TAKEAWAY

Just because you don't like it doesn't mean it doesn't have value for you and your business.

 ACTION

Take the time to understand it. Commit to a couple of hours and click around. Don't do anything specific. Just observe.

 TIP

Hire someone to show you what you need to know to further your initiatives.

 OBSERVATION

Everyone starts out not knowing what to do. It's OK. Making a concerted effort to being more informed and learning is the key.

Depending on your role and desired outcomes, you may need to learn different areas. For example, some recruiters are ninjas on LinkedIn Recruiter but completely neglect their own LinkedIn profile, how they show up, and even how to use LinkedIn.com. That's a huge miss.

CHAPTER 2

You According to Google

STANDOUT

Elevate your presence with purpose and clarity.

My guess is that like so many others, you go to Google when you need an answer to a question or more information on a particular topic. It's where people go to vet and verify.

Call it social proof if you prefer. Regardless, people want to know who you are, what you stand for, and who you know before returning your call, connecting with you, meeting up, buying, or working for or with you.

Have you Googled yourself lately?

It's the first exercise I do in all of our workshops.

Why? There are immediate observations and takeaways.

You may not use LinkedIn. However, Google may display your LinkedIn profile on page one of the results, depending on your name.

If you share your name with a celebrity, author, athlete, or lots of other people, you may not show up on page one. If that's the case, add your company name or city to the search terms.

LinkedIn is relevant to Google, the world's largest search engine. Google processes more than 3.5 billion searches per day.

Google sees LinkedIn as an authoritative site. You gain greater exposure and higher results because you're a LinkedIn member. Good, right?

Well, only if you have built out a compelling, relevant, and optimized LinkedIn profile. Yes, this is subjective, but it may not need to be.

What does that mean?

Is there enough information about you to create an excellent first impression? Does the information on Google, and most importantly LinkedIn, provide positive context for you, your work, or your business?

Is your LinkedIn profile unique to you? Or could it be plopped onto hundreds or thousands of other people's profiles?

Are people left wondering what you do and who you are? Are they underwhelmed by the lack of transparency, detail, clarity?

Would you be satisfied or impressed if you didn't know you?

Remember, all the context is to crystalize who you are, not confuse people.

There are plenty of people who have multiple companies, gigs. That works and will probably be more popular in the years ahead.

Can you explain how you manage those businesses, projects, consulting engagements? Why that particular combination?

The connective tissue is critical to create and establish a larger personal brand that makes sense to others and establishes you as an expert.

Still not sure?

Have you noticed that when you read an article or listen to a podcast how often the writer refers to a person's LinkedIn profile? I often see this reference from trusted publishers, including the *Wall Street Journal, Forbes,* and *Inc.* magazine. And they're not just referencing CEOs.

According to many people, LinkedIn is a definitive benchmark for vetting and verifying a person's professional and working background. So while it may not be your thing, it IS a thing to:

- Journalists, reporters, bloggers, podcasters
- Investors
- Members
- Donors
- Clients, buyers, prospects
- Candidates
- Talent

TAKEAWAYS

How you appear online is the foundation for how the world sees you.

You may not be able to control what shows up and in what order.

Strengthen your online presence by managing the content you create, post, and share. Align your online presence with the in-person you, including your values, professional expertise, and aspirations.

ACTION

Google yourself.

Do you show up on the first page of results?

TIP

Open an incognito window in Chrome or go to private mode in other browsers to disable your personal browsing history and the web cache. The results you receive are what everybody else would see.

If you share your name with a number of other people or a celebrity, author, or artist, add in your city or current organization to further refine your search.

OBSERVATION

What do you notice about what appears for you?

If LinkedIn is a top result, click the link to your profile.

How do you look?

Write down your reaction.

What should your profile and your online presence convey?

CHAPTER 3

Paranoid, Private, or Confident?

STANDOUT

Approach your business and career with confidence.

A small business owner called me not too long ago a bit alarmed and somewhat annoyed that LinkedIn was sending messages to his employees about jobs they might be interested in.

No doubt his concern is legitimate and this is a topic we hear a good deal about from other CEOs and business leaders. The smaller the business, the more this may be a problem.

If you own a small business, you understand the situation. You bring someone in, train them, give them a great opportunity, mentor them, and help them build their skills only to see them leave for a better opportunity. The beauty was that often these employees were in the trenches—heads-down working, not out meeting and networking with access to the larger world of people, potential, and opportunity.

That's changed. People are now visible through various networks.

People are sharing job openings with their professional and personal networks. Recruiters are searching for and reaching out to people. ***Top talent will always be recruited***. Today's social sharing just makes it quicker and more intentional.

While I nod and agree on the dislike of social media and the often ill effects it has on so many areas of our lives, LinkedIn is different and should be used differently.

Is your paranoia grounded? Maybe.

As a CEO, you have to decide where there's a greater upside. Is it better to keep your employees under the radar? Or is it better to have them look great (you did hire them because they were great, right?) and let your customers and prospects see what a rock-star team you've built? I'm not sure about you, but as a small business owner, I'm going with wanting them to look great. Great employees make you look smart—they build confidence with clients, especially in smaller businesses where clients know you can't possibly manage everything.

Considering the fact that you can't tell your employees that they can't be on LinkedIn or any other platform (remember, you don't own their profiles), you will look paranoid if you tell them not to have a profile or you try to manage their profile.

Turn your employees into ambassadors.

Make them a part of your social-business initiative.

- Ask them who they know

- Encourage them to reach out for both business development and recruiting purposes

- Give them a voice through content writing and sharing content

Explain your marketing strategy and how you've invested in content so they can share that information with others in their network. Explain why it's important that they are active.

Your employees are your greatest asset and you should want them to look good and know how to use the business tools that can increase their presence and your business.

In Reid Hoffman's most recent book, *The Alliance*, he talks about managing talent in a networked age and how it's time to rethink the employment model. I've come to see the value in this thinking and highly recommend the read. His book has never been more relevant and is worthy of reading and studying.

In the end, LinkedIn or any social platform or networking site is not the reason someone will leave your organization. It may make it seem that way but you may be fooling yourself more than anything.

One of the top reasons that people leave an organization is because of their manager.

It's time to be a **STANDOUT** employer and encourage **STANDOUT** employees.

Encouraging people to become engaged ambassadors who are proud of the company and for whom they work creates positive energy in your people and turns them into engaged ambassadors. A new energy and larger purpose might emerge.

Individuals seeking new business opportunities, jobs, internships:

- Where do you think people will look first when researching you?

- Do you think you can get away with being under the radar?

- Do you think people will wonder why you have no network?

- How will people get to know you quickly and accurately?

Once again, you decide if you want to be under the radar (you can still showcase yourself on LinkedIn and adjust particular settings) and be seen or come across with an anemic profile.

I am not sure why anyone would purposefully downplay their experience, skills, and network. There are so many ways to enhance what shows up and how you come across online.

TAKEAWAY

You represent your organization. Represent yourself and your organization well.

ACTION

Take a few minutes and review how your team looks online. What do they say about themselves and your organization?

TIP

Create straightforward guidelines for how you and your team should appear on LinkedIn and other social media platforms. Communicate your expectations and guidelines regularly so everyone is aware and clear.

OBSERVATION

Lead by example. Show everyone in your organization that you believe in the importance of showing up professionally and building strategic networks so marketing, business development, and recruiting is a natural extension of how people work.

CHAPTER 4

Learning Keeps You Relevant

STANDOUT

Realize you are always in beta mode; learning and growing are ongoing and critical to business and career success.

The access to learning and enhancing your skill set is easier than ever. And more necessary than ever.

I'm now choosing books, podcasts, and training based on when it was created; pre- or post-COVID-19. I believe we will view the world and everything in it from this point in history.

The old days are so far gone from our short-term memory, it's frightening. I have to remember how to go places, engage with others in public, and learn to smile with my eyes and hands. A wave and Zoom call have new meanings.

Conversations are richer from the start, sprinkled with children needing help with their online class or forgotten password, dogs barking at the approaching delivery driver, and the incessant sound of neighbors mowing their lawn and trimming their hedges.

The world as we know it today and from here on is a new world that demands new navigation. Employees need to juggle children, bosses, colleagues, and clients with diplomacy, patience, and grace.

They will also need to learn faster and more often than ever. They need to be several steps ahead, not one or two. We are called to think and act differently.

Months into COVID-19, it's time that everyone knows how to Zoom, schedule calls with a scheduling tool, use their CRM, and so much more.

If not now, when?

Regarding Zoom fatigue (or, whatever your video platform of choice is), I get it. However, is that fatigue worse than your daily commute, especially if you live in a metro area? As someone who is on Zoom every workday, yes, it's a lot. However, it sure beats driving around the Baltimore or D.C. beltways even a couple of times a week or jumping on airplanes two to four days a week.

Strategic Just Not So Tech Savvy

I've been known to change up in-person seating arrangements when I recognize that a Boomer would benefit from sitting next to a young Millennial or Gen Z. The Millennial or Gen Z keeps the Boomer moving by helping them along, showing them the button to push or where we are on the screen.

The Boomers get the strategy but many (not all) aren't comfortable with being online and pushing the buttons.

And often CEOs tell me they hand off LinkedIn to their marketing coordinator or social media person because they are young and "know all that stuff."

I get it. Think again though. Would you send them to an important meeting with a new or current client?

I didn't think so.

My friend Hollis Thomases wrote "11 Reasons a 23-Year-Old Shouldn't Run Your Social Media," a must-read article on why knowing the buttons isn't the reason to choose someone to manage LinkedIn and your social media. In the article, Hollis details 11 reasons why you don't want to hand it off without clear understanding and clarification.

1. They're not mature enough.
2. They may be focused on their own social media activity.
3. They may not have the same etiquette — or experience.
4. You can't control their friends.
5. No class can replace on-the-job training.
6. They may not understand your business.
7. Communication skills are critical.
8. Humor is tricky business.
9. Social media savvy is not the same as technical savvy.
10. Social media management can become crisis management.
11. You need to keep the keys.

I couldn't agree more.

By the way, don't date yourself. Don't get carried away with your own type of cool. I see far too many Boomers trying to be cool with emojis and slang and it just falls flat, especially when you're talking to a younger audience.

We also see some messages that are so stilted and formal they are uncomfortable to read. Save the "dear" or old English for a handwritten note. Just be professionally conversational.

Some clients have told us they like to have a typo in their message to make it look more realistic. I do NOT agree with this at all. Typos and grammatical errors happen to the best of us, but to do it intentionally and think it's a good strategy is just way off base. They fall into my "no need to respond" column.

Tech Savvy

While Gen Zers know the buttons, they may not fully know or understand your business, and usually don't know LinkedIn at all. It's certainly not their platform of choice and they don't realize that strategy is involved.

I've trained and coached many marketing coordinators who quietly admit on the first call that they have no idea what to do on LinkedIn but have to figure it out quickly because they were just put in charge of it.

Because they are comfortable online using multiple devices and knowing the shortcuts, they just need to learn the strategy and process and they are off and running.

Trained, they are mighty. Left to their own devices, you, your approach, and outcomes will falter.

Tech Savvy and Strategic

The third group is in between: older Millennials and Gen Xers. Probably 70% of this group know the buttons and the strategy and they just need to know how to leverage the newest features in LinkedIn, Sales Navigator, and Recruiter and they're off making things happen.

The balance of this group, the other 30%, was building their career and/or family, coaching soccer and lacrosse, and they missed LinkedIn pretty much entirely. They just didn't have the time or inclination to learn it. They are really more like the Boomers than they realize.

Understanding helps determine how to train and coach most effectively.

It's why when I'm leading a workshop for CEOs, I encourage them to bring their sales, marketing, and recruiting people because they are the people who typically are in there every day.

Ultimately though, it's critical that everyone ups their game, gets comfortable online, and uses the tools that provide brief but accurate communication online.

If you recognize that texting and messaging through LinkedIn is not your thing, consider using Grammarly to show you where your typos are or use the audio feature in your LinkedIn.com app to send a message. (Please double check it before sending.)

There are workarounds to ensure you don't send grammar bombs to people who ideally could be your next client, customer, or hire.

Know where you are. It's OK. What's important is moving forward. Practice.

My Girlfriend's on Facebook

I'd be remiss if I didn't mention a subset of older Millennials, mostly men, who are not fans of any social media, and they have thrown LinkedIn into that pile. When I talk with them, I realize that they were graduating when Facebook launched (February 2004) and so they missed the whole idea. LinkedIn launched later in 2004 and, like many emerging professionals, they didn't see the point, especially if they landed a job right out of university.

They do feel compelled to tell me that they aren't on social media, but their girlfriends or wives are. While I appreciate their perspective, they may be missing important business and career opportunities.

We need to mix everyone up so they can learn from one another and we can show them the value, the opportunity.

Every coach and trainer needs to remind people that learning is the only option and the best way to build a long-term career and business.

All I ever ask is that people come to a conversation with an open mind. This is the perpetual beta mindset that is critical these days. Don't underestimate your ability to learn and master new ideas and ways of working. Many of our clients are 60+ and they are active learners.

 TAKEAWAY

Ongoing learning is no longer optional if you have career aspirations or lead a team, unit, organization, or business.

 ACTION

Decide where you are on the continuum. Determine what you need to know and make a plan to achieve it.

 TIP

Know how you learn best and surround yourself with people, classes, or resources that will help you decrease your learning curve.

 OBSERVATION

Everyone is in the same place. Everyone needs to strengthen their skill set, and understand and serve as their own personal development champion.

CHAPTER 5

Go Beyond the Status Quo

STANDOUT

Pursue opportunities with tenacity. Seek to expand your career with the highest level of authenticity and care.

There are parts of this book I've wrestled with, knew needed to be discussed, but also recognized that I could not deliver with authenticity because they are not what I've experienced.

I've given deliberate thought and consideration to this chapter and I know not everyone's viewpoint or experience is represented. It's my hope and intention that as you read this chapter in its entirety, you consider your experience, bias, and focus moving forward.

Our consultant Des McCabe, an internationally recognized licensing specialist and author of the bestselling book *Work It Out!* challenged me on this topic. In order to change something you must change the energy. In this context and for this book, you and your community of connections are the energy.

Des said, "If I was training a group of people who had not worked in quite some time, I wouldn't put them in a room together with no one else. They'd look around and simply see themselves. I would put them in a room with people who were working. People with different careers and aspirations. People with different backgrounds and experiences. I'd mix them all up and create a new energy for them to work from."

Brilliant.

It's why this chapter is important. People's experiences need to be contemplated and understood. We can make a significant difference for ourselves, our organizations, and others in our community or network by pushing beyond the status quo, introducing, sponsoring, mentoring, and hiring with intention.

As an individual, you must show up, engage, and push beyond your known community, geography, and limiting beliefs to create a new community that provides you with an entree to new people so that you can pursue new opportunities and relationships that propel you forward.

As a woman, I can write about women even as my experiences may be different. I talk with and hear from young women who are just starting their career as well as women who have blazed amazing professional trails. Often their comments are similar, eerily similar.

On the following pages, I'd like to explore the importance of recognizing where you are today, where you hope and need to go, and how the status quo has evaporated for good. Throughout the world, the status quo has smacked up against massive disruption.

Much of the data, including LinkedIn's, is pre-COVID, and with such rampant change, referencing it may not provide relevance. It's why I will benchmark based on recent articles in the *Wall Street Journal* and LinkedIn.

Diversity in the workplace

In LinkedIn's September 2020 U.S. Workforce Report, they report that:

- Over 169 million workers in the U.S. have LinkedIn profiles

- Over 20,000 companies in the U.S. use LinkedIn to recruit

- Over 3 million jobs are posted on LinkedIn in the U.S. every month

- Members can add over 36,000 skills to their profiles to showcase their professional brands

On September 28, 2020, Te-Ping Chen's article, "Why Are There Still So Few Black CEOs?" cites that out of the chief executives running America's top 500 companies, just 1%, or four, are Black. The numbers aren't much better on the rungs of the ladder leading to that role. Among all U.S. companies with 100 or more employees, Black people hold just 3% of executive or senior-level roles, according to Equal Employment Opportunity Commission data.

Chen goes on to say that many companies tend to emphasize diversity in recruitment but overlook retention and advancement, researchers and executives say. And while companies have long talked about the importance of diversity—spending billions a year on such efforts—money has often been devoted to flawed programs such as diversity training which show only mixed evidence of effectiveness.

Black employees are missing in the all-important pipeline of talent that feeds the CEO job. An April Stanford Graduate School of Business study found that in the Fortune 100, which are a mix of public and privately held companies, Black executives hold just 3% of the profit-and-loss positions in the C-suite that are key to company success and are often seen as a prerequisite to the top job.

The study found that when Black employees are elevated to the C-suite, they are frequently given roles with less advancement potential, such as chief human resources officer, chief sales officer or chief administration executive: Black people hold 13%, 20% and 43% of such roles in the Fortune 100, respectively.

The ranks of Black chief executives have stayed low even as other ethnic minorities have seen greater, albeit still limited, advancement. Among CEOs of S&P 500 companies, 11% are ethnic minorities. Of the total, 3% are Latino, 3% are Indian, 2% are Asian, 1% are Middle Eastern and 1% are multiracial. Just 1% are Black, according to an analysis by MyLogIQ, a data tracker. Black people make up about 13% of the U.S. population.

Does this apply to women?

Lauren Weber and Vanessa Fuhrmans' *WSJ* article, "How the Coronavirus Crisis Threatens to Set Back Women's Careers," illustrates the effect the pandemic is having on women.

The authors say, "A comprehensive new study by McKinsey and LeanIn.org suggests that many women—especially mothers—may have to step back or away from jobs because of the pandemic's impact on their lives."

Women have already lost a disproportionate number of jobs. That is partly because of a segregated workforce in many fields in which women make up more of the lower-income service and retail jobs that vanished as COVID-19 gripped the economy. While women are 47% of the U.S. labor force, they accounted for 54% of initial coronavirus-related job losses and still make up 49% of them, according to McKinsey & Co.

Though the pandemic has forced fathers and mothers to juggle careers with child care and remote schooling, women often shoulder the brunt of those responsibilities.

That outsize burden has long-term consequences. About one in five working mothers surveyed this summer for the sixth annual

Women in the Workplace study by McKinsey and LeanIn.org say they are considering dropping out of the workforce, at least temporarily—compared with 11% of fathers. An additional 15% of mothers report they may dial back their careers, either by cutting their hours or switching to a less demanding role. Among women with young children, the struggle is especially acute: nearly a quarter say they may take a leave of absence or quit altogether.

Nor is the parental load the only factor. Among childless men and women, 10% also say they are considering leaving the workforce and across the board, employees are more likely to cite burnout and anxiety over job security as their biggest work challenge other than child care. Black women are even more likely than women overall to consider downshifting or taking a leave from work and cite health concerns as a reason, the report says.

The findings come from one of the most comprehensive pandemic-era surveys of working women and men in which researchers at McKinsey and LeanIn.org polled more than 40,000 North American employees. If employers don't take more action to shore up mothers in their jobs, McKinsey and LeanIn warn, they could see the percentage gains women have made over the past several years up and down the management ladder dissipate.

Thinking of starting a business?

In Gwynn Guilford and Charity L. Scott's *WSJ* article, "Is It Insane to Start a Business During Coronavirus? Millions of Americans Don't Think So," the reporters showcase the number of people starting new businesses.

Applications for the employer identification numbers that entrepreneurs need to start a business have passed 3.2 million so far this year, compared with 2.7 million at the same point in 2019, according to the U.S. Census Bureau. That group includes gig-economy workers and other independent contractors who may have struck out on their own after being laid off.

Even excluding those applicants, new filings among a subset of business owners who tend to employ other workers reached 1.1 million through mid-September, a 12% increase over the same period last year and the most since 2007, the data shows.

Graduating seniors are now experiencing unexpected difficulties finding their first job or the internship that often led to their first job. The added disadvantage they face is that they typically haven't built a strong professional network to help them. For them, we recommend diving deeper into their alumni network. This is a must-do for students and emerging professionals.

Over the last few months, I have had a number of conversations with people whose experiences reflect what the *WSJ* has reported. It's real and it's difficult and sometimes immobilizing for those who have experienced bias.

One of the most personal and significant conversations that I've had over the past year was with someone I consider one of the most positive, driven, and committed entrepreneurs I know. Our conversation expanded my thinking and perspective.

A conversation with Edwin Avent.
Edwin and I met in 2005 when our paths crossed in the local Baltimore publishing world. Back then we'd sit in Edwin's office and talk about magazine publishing, building an online presence, and the highs and lows of being an entrepreneur.

Over the years, while connected on LinkedIn, we lost track. When we reconnected at a local event in late 2019, we committed to following up and arranging a call.

I was completely undone by our conversation. Edwin's perspective and the depth of our conversation stunned me. I hung up not sure what to do next.

The conversation convicted me for months. The intensity in his voice stirred my thinking and stayed with me.

The holidays came and went. I was off to a conference, the pandemic broke out. I was focused on keeping our team and family healthy. I never followed up. Social unrest erupted and almost every day I was reminded of my conversation with Edwin.

Finally, I messaged him hoping we could talk again. Graciously, Edwin responded and our 30-minute conversation lasted two hours. Edwin was real, concerned, angry, and equally optimistic and hopeful.

We talked at length, as we did in the fall of 2019, about the lack of opportunities for Black men, how the Ivy League network and fraternity network hadn't provided the opportunities others have realized, and how the C-Suite's doors just haven't opened up to Black men.

While it's positive to build board diversity, it's not the same as running the business. The work that Edwin does in the community as the Chair of the Board of Trustees for the Baltimore Collegiate School for Boys is one example of his personal mission to help Black men change the trajectory of their lives.

Isn't he exactly the kind of person you want leading your organization? Shouldn't this kind of experience speak to how he can lead and contribute to the greater good and growth of a mission-oriented organization or high-growth business?

The same is true of women. If a woman as mother, care partner, online teacher, leader, high-contributor, manager, or doer is committed to all of the areas of her life, shouldn't we afford her the ability to manage those commitments with a degree of grace and flexibility?

Your role in creating a diverse workforce.

I encourage you to build out a diverse community of connections that enables you to be more effective at building your career and helping others.

To everyone hiring, it's your responsibility to create the best team of people possible. Study the data and you will learn that diverse teams benefit people and the bottom line.

In light of Des' comment, our collective stories, and our direct and indirect experiences, can we expand not only our network, community, and opportunities but our hearts as well? The end result will be stronger and more representative teams and communities.

Can we, as Des shared with us, build bridges not barriers, collaboration not competition, and create leverage not limits?

I think we can. The marketplace is a great place to create opportunity for all. If we don't, who will?

People's stories are unique and yet universal. Both are true. Everyone seeks to realize a dream, an opportunity, or relationship that gives shape and meaning to their lives. My observations are my own and from people I have spoken with and worked alongside. I do not claim to be an expert or position myself as an authority on diversity and inclusion.

TAKEAWAY

Create an online presence and network that is diverse and positions you for the career you aspire to.

ACTION

Consider and connect with the people who can help you find opportunities where you can add your talent, skills, and experiences.

TIP

Build your network with purpose. Let people know why you are connecting with them. Be clear about how they can help you and how you can return the favor.

OBSERVATION

Never stop expanding and cultivating your network and pursuing those ideal opportunities.

CHAPTER 6

You Are More Than Your Bio

STANDOUT

*Create context and showcase your experience,
skills, talent, and community contributions.*

You may not think that you've lived a remarkable and storied life or career. Most people don't. The crazy thing is that most people who have don't even see their magic and awesomeness. How can that be true?

They, like you, see themselves as quite usual and even ordinary.

You may wonder how I know this. Over the last several years, we've written thousands of LinkedIn profiles for CEOs, business owners, executive consultants, authors, sales professionals, marketers, job seekers, and others.

My team and I have interviewed each person and we've listened to their stories: what propels them to do great work, why they believe what they believe. We hear them talk about the legacy they hope to leave for their families, communities, and industry.

(Oh, yes, of course, there are some gigantic egos out there. However, I'm not writing this for them. They have publicists and marketing engines devoted to promoting their every word.)

You may have a resumé and a bio, but do you have your story written in the first person in a way that tells the world who you are and why they should know you?

I submit that resumés are pretty old school, so early 21st century. Do we even need them?

I'm not sure I've ever read a resumé and thought, I must get to know this person. This person is fantastic. This person will help us grow our business, expand our offerings, increase our profitability, etc.

Actually knowing the person is what's critical. Understanding how they're wired, what they're like, the type of culture where they thrive, how they lead and talk to others will determine whether they can be successful in a particular job or company.

Telling your story matters.

You may not be a writer.
Only you can tell your story. That doesn't mean you need to write it. It means you need to share it with someone who can write it for you. You need to provide the background—the why and how.

If you are a young professional and don't have experience or skills, think beyond your experiences and think about what you gained in school, community service, traveling, and your family and interests.

Think about your strengths and those oh-so-necessary soft skills.

Consider your passions: music, athletics, arts, etc., and weave them into your story.

Are you beginning to see how no one else can capture the essence of you?

Are you the second, third, fourth generation or more in your family business? You have a story ready to go!

Maybe you served in the military. There is an inherent richness to what you convey. What prompted you to choose the military? Even your choice of military branch provides a glimpse into who you are.

Perhaps you've had several jobs, multiple careers, and don't see how they come together. Think about your agility, always learning something new, optimism, and the ability to manage risk. Those are needed qualities and strengths for business and mission-oriented endeavors.

Maybe you traveled to a new country, learned the language, built a business, or found success within a company that values you. That's a great story.

Compelling stories are all around us. Begin to capture and share yours.

TAKEAWAY

You are the only person who can tell your story in a meaningful way.

While the facts are necessary, telling your story and your "why" is far more relevant and interesting to the person learning about you.

ACTION

Answer these questions:

- What do you do?

- Why do you do the work you do?

- What separates you from your peers and competitors?

- Who is your primary audience? Recruiters, prospects, investors, etc.

Use your answers to develop your profile, resume, bio, personal mission statement, etc.

TIP

Most people, unless you're a professional writer, need an editor. Ask someone else to review, critique, and provide feedback.

OBSERVATION

The best personal stories and profiles are first-person, written for the primary audience you are seeking to attract, aren't all "I" statements, and demonstrate expertise, personality, and a genuine sense of who you are.

CHAPTER 7

You Are More Than Influential: You Are Significant

STANDOUT

Thrive by supporting and serving others.

"Can we schedule time to talk about LinkedIn algorithms? My views are down. I can't figure out why some things do well and others fall flat."

There are a couple of reasons I sigh when I read emails like this. None of us, even the most statistically minded uber LinkedIn users know LinkedIn's algorithm definitively. And, if they do, they also know it will change and they will have to run their algorithmic race all over again.

This is true of Google, Facebook, and others. In their pursuit of power and market share, they must be a few steps ahead of their competitors and users.

If that's the case, and it's my assertion that it is, then what?

Follow best practices, aim higher, and do what we learned long ago. Develop relationships that further your aspirations and career, short and long term.

Get to know people and be known.

Best Opening Line
"How can I serve you?"

Now that's a question that stopped me and made me think. It wasn't, "Who do you want to know?" or "Who can I introduce you to?" or "How can I help you?"

All well-intentioned questions for sure.

"How can I serve you?" is strong and humble and bold. That's what I recall thinking. That question came at the 28-minute mark in a 30-minute conversation with Joseph DeMattos, Jr., Executive Director of Health Facilities of Maryland (HFAM) and the CEO of Triple Latte Leadership (yes, he loves coffee).

It had been five years since we last spoke and in 30 minutes, I remembered how easy he was to talk to, how committed he is to his work and members, and his deep commitment to serving others and leading with integrity.

When I mentioned his name later the same day to a client, her response was, "He is just the best guy."

It's good to be known.

Ed Mullin, the CIO/VP of Think is similar. He has deep networks in tech, startups, robotics, and nonprofits, and has one of the largest social graphs in Baltimore.

He is continually doing. From finding laptops and devices for students so they can learn remotely during the pandemic to advocating throughout Maryland for STEM, and from advancing networking for high school students from his alma mater to solving challenging technology and productivity problems for clients, Ed is well known among his connections.

One of the reasons our business exists is because Ed saw our vision for empowering others to embrace LinkedIn for their branding, business development, and recruiting efforts, and invited me to speak at as many networking events as he hosted. His referrals and introductions opened doors to conversations and business. No selling needed.

I remember talking with Ed one day and expressing my gratitude for yet another referral and remarking that I couldn't possibly create as many introductions for him and his company. He laughed and said, "No worries. Everytime I introduce someone to you and you help them or give them the guidance they need, you make me look smart. That's enough for me."

It's good to be known.

Having go-to people are key professionally. David Nour, CEO of The Nour Group calls this group of people your 2 a.m. people. Who are the people that you could call at 2 a.m. and they would answer? His presentation on relationships is one of the best talks I have ever heard and it resonated with me.

We need to build our 2 a.m. club. It doesn't need to be large. It needs to be significant.

We should be a part of other people's 2 a.m. club, too.

When we talk to clients, we refer to these people as Centers of Influence (COI). They know, like, and trust you. You know, like, and trust them. They have good networks and are connectors. Of course, we appreciate when those COIs have strong LinkedIn networks so we can tap into the power of 2nd degree connections for our clients.

Jim Ries, the Director of Business Development at Offit Kurman, is a COI who is masterful at connecting people and follow up. He meets, he connects, he arranges a Zoom/phone/meeting (this is mid-2020, that's the right order at the moment), and he learns about the person. He talks with them, asks questions, and knows who he can introduce them to. The funny thing is, he's not a name dropper. You know those folks, right? Always talking up who they know and asking if you know them and then offering to introduce you.

That's not Jim. Maybe he makes a lot of notes or maybe he's built incredible muscle memory for people. He knows who you should know.

And there are others I've never met in person. However, we've developed a knowing, a friendship, a collegial relationship and I value these people deeply. Throughout the country and really the world, I've connected with amazing people doing important work in a myriad of ways and industries.

Many of these people have come from my work with Vistage, the world's largest CEO peer advisory organization. Over the years, my team and I have had the privilege of working with Vistage as an instructor, speaker to their groups, and resource for helping their Chairs engage with leaders in their respective markets.

This book would not be complete though without sharing my Bob Miller story. It is undeniably my favorite LinkedIn story. Not too long ago, I found the email that cued up my most unlikely friendship with the world's greatest sales trainer.

The email served as an informal introduction to Bob Miller with a mention to take extra special care of him. I realized he was important to the person introducing us.

Before I had the chance to call him, he called me. There is so much to say about the friendship that emerged over time from helping

Bob with his LinkedIn profile. If I went into too much detail, this book would be a different story, so I will instead share the blog post I wrote after Bob died in the fall of 2017.

A Tribute to Bob Miller —
An Unexpected Mentor and Friend
Published on November 2, 2017

This post is more tribute than blog post. It's a story about an unlikely friendship, somewhat random at best but one rich with inspired conversation, thoughtful mentoring, and mutual respect.

In October 2015, I was sitting in a client's office in San Diego when I answered the phone and heard a rather gravelly voice say, "Hello, Colleen. This is Bob Miller. Do you know who I am?"

Clearly realizing I should, I quickly quipped, "Well there's probably more than one of you. Which one are you?"

"Ever heard of Miller Heiman?"

"Yes, of course."

"I am that Bob Miller."

"Ahhh, oh, but of course."

"I need a LinkedIn profile and I heard I should talk with you. Can you help me?"

"Yes, of course."

And, with that exchange an unlikely friendship was underway. Interviewing Bob for his LinkedIn profile was clearly a career highlight. The more he talked, the more mesmerized I was. It was a bit like a child at the knee of a master storyteller. I loved his stories, his metaphors, and his understanding of how sales has had to adapt to a modern buyer. He believed, and I wholeheartedly agreed, that a company's guiding principles, process, and pursuit of excellence will continue to differentiate them online and offline.

When we reviewed all the people who sent him LinkedIn connection requests (and there were hundreds), they were personalized with comments like:

> *"You changed how I worked and sold. You helped me increase my success and provide for my family like I could never have imagined."*

> *"Bob, Over the years I have read and reread all your books. Thank you. You have made me a better salesperson and leader."*

They went on and on. And, he always seemed a bit humbled by these remarks from people who were virtual strangers but had been educated, inspired, informed, and encouraged by his work and insight. A true master of sales and more importantly, people.

In his humility, there was confidence and a sense of accomplishment. He knew his work transformed how others saw themselves and the work they did. I think, if nothing else, he made salespeople proud to be sales professionals.

Repeatedly, he told me he loved the work we were doing at Intero and how our consulting team helps clients redefine selling and servicing their customers. Once we finished his profile, we continued to talk via email and phone. He would call, and regardless of what I was doing, I took the call. Who would send a call from the world's greatest sales trainer to voicemail?

Not me. Our conversations covered his history, current health, coaching clients, and our business. He was curious and continued to remind me about guiding principles, process, and people. He asked pointed questions and challenged my thinking. He pointed out landmines when I shared opportunities that crossed my path.

He listened. He sent articles and personal writings to help me think through the upside and downside of various opportunities. He settled my thinking and strengthened my decision making. Subsequent conversations let me know that if we were in the same room, he would give me a high five, fist bump, or perhaps even a bear hug.

Throughout 2017, we had deep conversations about end of life and owning your own journey. We had several of these conversations as I sat with my mother during her hospice stay. They were beautiful days actually and I realized he was helping me think through my own mother's end of life experience. Bob was bold and ready for whatever faced him, and unafraid he said, time and time again. We laughed a lot in our conversations that year and he continued to regale me with sales stories, his successes, and even some of the failures he faced. Even Bob Miller had a couple of those, too.

As I scrolled through our messages this week, this (my favorite) jumped out. Certainly, this may go down as one of my favorite LinkedIn messages ever.

Jan 28

 Colleen -You are incredible! Thank you so very much. I cannot begin to tell you how much I appreciate your input. Very, very helpful. What a wonderful and oh-so-kind gift with which you have blessed me. It is difficult for me to comprehend what good friends we have become without ever meeting face-to-face! My warmest and affectionate regards, Bob

1:58 PM

The crazy part? **We never met.** Over the last six and a half years, I have met some of America's best leaders. I have had the opportunity to talk with, learn about and from serial entrepreneurs, executive coaches, CEOs, and business owners who are committed to building great companies for their employees and their customers. I have met most of them through or as a result of LinkedIn.

When people tell me LinkedIn is not worth their time or effort, I laugh and think of Bob. I think about the man who unabashedly claimed to be the best-known sales coach on planet Earth, and how, while he was discriminating about his connections, he saw the value of building a network where you could share your expertise and knowledge with others.

In May of 2017, I was in Walnut Creek and we planned on getting together for dinner but he had a fall and had to head to the hospital. It wasn't meant to be. Nonetheless, over that summer, we spent hours on the phone evaluating business opportunities.

At 85, he had probably forgotten more than most people know and was as sharp as anyone half his age. He described and recalled stories of people, places, and experiences that helped me better understand how to evaluate and think about my business and its path moving forward.

Every few weeks I would receive or send off an email. On September 19th, I sent my last email to Bob.

It was unusual not to hear back within a day or two. Still, I thought he might be traveling or visiting one of his sons. And so, when I received an email from his son a few days later, I knew what this email meant.

I am confident Bob had all the tough conversations he needed to have. He appreciated every sunny California day and relished the work and passion he shared with so many.

As I reflect on this unlikely friendship, the sweet conversations and all the mentoring, I am feeling grateful for Bob Miller and how serendipitous and fabulous the world can be.

Note: Bob Miller's obituary appears on his LinkedIn profile and the comments from so many continue to serve as a testament to his legacy.

Significance, a noun, is the quality of being worthy of attention; importance. This is a goal worthy of your investment and energy. The quick hit of social influence is fleeting while significance is the real deal.

When people tell me there is no way to develop strong relationships online, I always share my Bob Miller story. Over the years and maybe even more now, I have met and cultivated friendships with so many people across the world.

TAKEAWAY

Social influence is often fleeting. 15 minutes in the sun. Aim for the long term. Go for significance.

ACTION

Consider where you are in your career and how you create significance. Are you leading, mentoring, speaking, writing, building deep relationships with family, friends, colleagues?

TIP

Map out and understand your various networks.

OBSERVATION

The pursuit of online algorithms is elusive and futile; significance is not.

Be a great and proactive connector.

CHAPTER 8

The Power of Weak Ties

STANDOUT

*Recognize that expanding a community of connections
unleashes more business and career opportunities.*

Maybe my mother was ahead of her time. She always told me that it's who you know, not what you know. At the time, I was a young woman in a small high school in Buffalo, New York. I'm not sure that statement had much influence on me.

Now, I consider her sentiment worthy of mentioning. I do believe that what you know is crucial to building a successful career and personal brand. My version of her philosophy is that it's who you know AND what you know.

Seeing Value

Today, your network is your currency, especially for those leading companies and in business development and sales. You are the face of your business or organization and you need to know people to open doors and hire the best talent. It's just that simple. People want to know who they are working with and for.

Embrace that and you can work with the best companies and hire top talent. Miss that and your metaphorical runway will be far longer as you will be less competitive than those who understand how to engage this way.

I met Dr. Philip Brown, the President & CEO of Phoenix Mecano North America through Monica Kolbay who leads and owns ArachnidWorks, Inc., a Maryland-based marketing firm. Monica mentioned in our first conversation that Philip saw enormous value and potential in LinkedIn and wanted his team to know more about how they could use it to connect with their customers and prospects.

When the CEO sees the value and vision for LinkedIn and endorses it, the team begins to see its importance. Conversely, the CEO who says, "Do it," but never does ultimately demonstrates that it's not important. If it's not important to leadership why would it be important to others?

Philip recently received his DBA (Doctor of Business Administration) from Hood College. His dissertation, "The Exploratory Data Analysis of Business-to-Business Quantitative Relationship-Value: An Intangible Exchange Asset Dimension" illustrates his interest in networks, connections, and their value.

During one of our early conversations, Philip mentioned his interest in the value of weak ties and Mark Sanford Granovetter's work on the topic. The keystone of his work is that in marketing, information science, or politics, **weak ties enable reaching populations and audiences that are not accessible via strong ties.**

Consider the levels of relationships in LinkedIn. First level connections are a combination of strong and weak ties. We like to identify your VERY strongest connections as Centers of Influence (COIs). From there, most people will determine that they have another layer of strong ties who are not COIs but are strong connections: people you know, talk with, or who you can reconnect with quite easily.

From there, you may have a number of first level connections you don't know.

Decide what to do about that. Here are some considerations based on your strategy for using LinkedIn and any social platform.

- Keep them in there and be more discerning going forward.

- Remove the very random people. Don't worry, they are NOT notified that you've removed them. They won't know they've been removed unless, of course, they do know you and notice that they are no longer connected with you.

The Who

Remember, LinkedIn looks at the relevancy of your network to pro-vide suggestions for new people who may be of interest.

Let's say you switch industries or geographies. If you've been in healthcare and have a lot of connections in the healthcare indus-try, LinkedIn is going to suggest more of those types of people. So, if you move to IT for example, you need to transition your network to people in IT or those working in IT companies.

Same with geographies. We work with lots of people who work regionally, nationally, or internationally and now they are trying to engage a very targeted geographic area. In order to do that, they have to jumpstart their network with a localized group of connec-tions preferably with larger networks.

While someone is a 1st level connection and you have access to them, it doesn't mean they are a strong tie. In fact, that's OK based on the research of weak ties. It's where there is a lot of opportunity.

People call us all the time saying they need new prospects and my first question is always the same: "Who are you currently connected to?" I guarantee there are opportunities within your first level net-work that with some nurturing will turn into business and career engagements.

The exercise of understanding your network is also valuable in seeing where you have gaps.

Want to know the single most startling gap for most people when they look closely at their network?

They are not connected to their clients/customers.

That is a wow to me every time and an immediate action item.

CEOs and small business owners: Shouldn't you be connected to your peers in your client companies?

I posit, absolutely.

Let's start by understanding 1st level connections and then we can begin to expand your network with 2nd level people.

Usually there will be a number of 2nd level connections that you actually know. Immediately turn them into 1st level. Why? It expands your network with more people who will probably help increase your network in the right way.

You want to connect with the people you know. It increases your visibility within an industry, geography, company, professional organization, group, etc.

See where we're going?

Just Say Hello

Larry Eason and I connected in 2011 through a group called LinkedIn for Good. We've talked a number of times over years, traded some introductions, and enjoy catching up every once in a while.

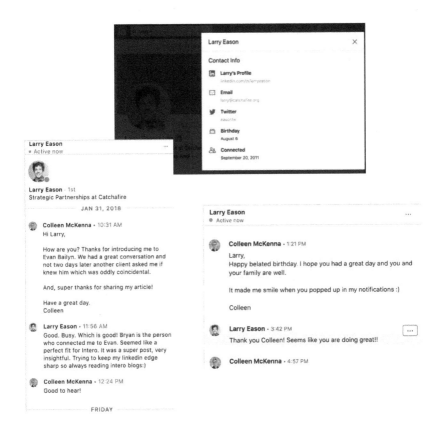

When I received a notification that it was Larry's birthday, I sent him a quick note wishing him well. We had a friendly exchange and it was good to reconnect with him.

Larry is someone I'm glad to know. He's a good person doing good work in the world. He's someone I want to know.

We all have these people in our lives and in our networks. These are the people we need to be more intentional about knowing and touching base with occasionally.

TAKEAWAY

While we love our Centers of Influence, we recognize the potential is unlimited. People you don't know can become powerful allies.

ACTION

Focus your efforts on developing weak ties by asking how you can serve them.

TIP

There are various levels of weak ties. Determine a few each week and initiate a conversation with them.

OBSERVATION

People want to serve and help others. Your job is to make it easy for them to do that on your behalf.

CHAPTER 9

The Relevancy of Your Network

STANDOUT
Become a Center of Influence.

"Do I connect with everyone?"

"I feel like if I don't get to 500 connections, people notice and think I don't know what I'm doing on LinkedIn. What do you think?"

"Can I be selective on LinkedIn? I prefer not to connect with people I don't know."

These are questions that nearly everyone asks during a call, training, or coaching session. They are great questions. My answer is usually the same.

It depends on why you're on LinkedIn.

Among my peers, I undoubtedly have one of the smallest networks. It's intentional.

It's not difficult to expand your network and have 20,000 or more connections.

LinkedIn maxes out your 1st level connections or network at 30,000. All your 1st level connections (as of this writing) are automatically your Followers. You can have additional Followers that are not connections.

Followers make sense and are an extension of LinkedIn's original Influencer program. In earlier years, LinkedIn invited thought leaders to write exclusive content for LinkedIn and all members could follow their content.

It's rare that someone with a large following and platform is managing their own LinkedIn and social media channels unless of course, they have a particular interest in being active on LinkedIn. This is certainly true for CEOs and leaders of large organizations.

Will connecting with them help you expand their network?

Maybe but my guess is their networks are quite broad and ultimately, not as helpful as you might think.

Relevance is dialed in

In a 2019 LinkedIn blog post, Pete Davies, former Senior Director of Project Management at LinkedIn, wrote about the relevancy on LinkedIn.

> *"We have a saying at LinkedIn: 'People You Know, Talking About Things You Care About.' This is, simply, how we think about the LinkedIn Feed.*
>
> *Our mission is to help people be more productive and successful, and it is what drives us daily.*
>
> *We strongly believe that people need their professional communities to help them along the way, whether that's current*

or former colleagues, peers in the same industry, or those that share similar interests or career ambitions.

The LinkedIn Feed is the home of these communities, and the conversations that happen within them."

The goal is to connect or reconnect you with people who can help you further your business or goal objectives or aspirations.

LinkedIn is designed to create community. The community you need.

Design and build your network accordingly.

Do you want a network of peers, influencers, referral partners, clients, prospects, potential talent, and industry thought leaders? Or do you want people you don't know and probably never will?

If you're in the business of recruiting, your strategy is to connect with as many people as possible or at least in a particular industry if you have a niche or industry focus.

For example, if you are an executive recruiter, it doesn't help you to have a lot of entry level or mid-level connections. You need C-level executives.

TAKEAWAY

Build a strategic network that matters to you. No one needs another address book or list of people who are completely unknown to them.

ACTION

Always focus on quality not quantity. Quantity is easy to achieve. Quality is not.

TIP

Cultivate your community of connections with care and feed them valuable insight so they keep you top of mind.

OBSERVATION

Never assume that you're connected to someone. Check, and if not, get connected. Often we overlook the most obvious people.

CHAPTER 10

Random or Purposeful?

STANDOUT

Understand how to build communities, not just connections.

I've led hundreds of workshops with CEOs and their leadership teams in a wide range of industries and stages of maturity. Inevitably, they share their thoughts on social media and LinkedIn. "Why do I get so many random invitations?" someone asked.

The general consensus is that they don't like constant, random invitations.

"By virtue of being the CEO, people want to know you and connect with you. You make the decisions and you authorize purchases," I answered. It comes with the title, period.

Other things I often hear when I'm leading a workshop for CEOs and business owners:

"I don't want to be a jerk but I get too many invitations from random salespeople to respond to."

"Is it better to just delete them or should I answer them?"

"They only want something from me. They're just trying to sell me something. Don't they know I already know a dozen financial planners, insurance people, printers, IT providers? I don't want them in my network trolling around."

There's truth in each of those statements. I get it. Let's take a look at what's happening in a typical invitation exchange.

For business development folks, salespeople and everyone who wants to talk with CEOs

Your job is to get in front of decision makers. Period. And now, you use LinkedIn. Think about your sales process. You have a quota, you have a list of prospects or customers and you need to make a certain number of calls, appointments, and actual meetings in a week and month. You are diligent, often aggressive (that's part of your DNA and job description if you are a hunter) and you reach out via every means possible.

If you were the CEO, would you take your call, respond to your email, accept your LinkedIn invitation?

Be honest. Have you provided enough reason, value, or earned enough trust to warrant his or her response? Do you have enough status, power, or known celebrity to warrant a CEO of a company to want to talk with you? If you are honest, probably not.

The best business development process is well crafted, intentional, and thoughtful. It's personalized through good research, an introduction, a great referral, and a proof-based value proposition.

Consider it from the CEO's perspective. They are smart people and have trusted go-to advisors. They probably have insurance, financial advice, printers, and most everything else it takes to run a business. Once again, why should they connect with you?

Colleen Stanley, president of SalesLeadership, a sales development firm specializing in the integration of emotional intelligence, sales and sales leadership skills, wrote an article titled, "Are You Thinking Like a CEO?" which speaks about this topic directly. CEOs know people, know how to reach out to those they want to do business with, and are careful about inviting new people in without a reference or referral. Initially, at least, you represent a learning curve, change, and risk.

Many of today's CEOs are not comfortable online. They did not necessarily come of age in a collaborative, open networking system. They are concerned about privacy, breaches, and the list goes on. Younger CEOs are far more likely to be open to connecting. Know your audience.

Everyone says start at the top. Sometimes it works but often it doesn't. Consider starting where you have a champion, a well-respected champion.

For CEOs

You are the person that business development people, salespeople, consultants, and job seekers need to reach. You can't possibly talk to everyone nor should you. You need to be discerning, no doubt, and you need to manage those parameters. But you may also need help, advice, new solutions, or products, and these business development/salespeople, consultants, and job seekers have what you may need. You may also need to replace a supplier for poor performance, inferior products and services, etc., or you may need to transition into systems, solutions, and products that did not exist a few years ago (CRM, marketing automation, content management system, etc.) and you need to vet your options.

Business development people and other folks are here to bridge the gap. Find the good ones and you are golden. Having a vetting process is important. One of the major reasons business development folks push to get in front of you is obvious. You are the final authority. You sign the checks.

You should want to better manage the flow of people reaching out to you on LinkedIn. If so, read on. There are ways to manage how you show up and whether people can reach you.

Three ways to earn trust and nurture your current network.

Ask for referrals. You may or may not receive them, but at least you asked. Consider who you are asking and why they would refer you. Have you treated them well? Most people don't ask for referrals even though they recognize it's the number one way of gaining new leads.

Be great, no, be amazing, at what you do. Do more than what is expected. Create a reputation that begins to precede you (find a market niche, for example). You will receive some good referrals.

Be *so* good, you receive referrals without asking for them. It's a bit like the Holy Grail, right? This is where you have earned the trust in an area, geography, market.

I listened closely to a presentation on proximity not long ago. While it related to a different topic, I saw the immediate connection to the value of proximity for people thinking about their career, leading a business or organization, or selling and marketing.

Proximity is defined as nearness in space, time, or relationship.

Everyone gets proximity, right?

Proximity directly relates to how close you are to your customers, prospects, influencers, connectors, and talent.

If you haven't considered the importance of proximity, consider these points:

- If you are known by others, you avail yourself of new opportunities.

- If people don't know you, they don't realize that they may be missing out on something important.

- If you and your business fall behind, it's harder and harder to catch up.

- If others gain and surpass you in recruiting and selling, it will become increasingly more difficult to hire the best talent or do business with the best companies.

Proximity is critical.

When people tell me they aren't interested in or don't need to use LinkedIn, what they really mean is that they don't think there is value in building business connections and networks. They aren't as concerned as they profess to be about recruiting, and they are willing to give up their position as an industry leader.

Proximity reveals your influence.

According to Demand Gen Report's 2014 B2B Buyer Behavior Survey

- 76% of people say they prefer to work with vendors recommended by someone they know

- 73% prefer to work with salespeople recommended by someone they know

Are there people I don't know well? Absolutely. Some I should know better? Absolutely.

TAKEAWAY

To build the most effective network and community for your career and business, purposeful always outpaces random.

ACTION

Decide to be more purposeful by personalizing and knowing who you are connecting and networking with and why.

TIP

Let people know you are specific about connecting to create business and career opportunities, not just to connect.

OBSERVATION

Decide how you want to build your network and community and then go for it.

CHAPTER 11

Personalize, Personalize, Personalize

STANDOUT

Always create an impression.

If I had a penny for every time I talk about personalizing connection requests, follow up messages, and introducing posts, there would be some extra zeros on my bank balance.

I recommend sending introductions and posts from your desktop or laptop rather than your phone. It's easier to write that extra sentence, you're less likely to have typos, and you can even take a messaging template and copy/paste.

If you're trying to grab someone's attention, spark a conversation, or attempt to build credibility and trust, **the easiest way to do that is to send a personalized message.**

This is especially true for business development and recruiting. If you want someone to eventually work with or for you, don't they deserve a personalized note?

If you saw them in person, would you just walk up to them and stand there?

Our former recruiter received an email from LinkedIn stating that she was in the top 1% of recruiters using LinkedIn Recruiter. Why? Her InMail response rate topped 45%. She was fanatical about her messaging and making sure she personalized as much and as creatively as she could.

Pause, don't click.
People say it slows them down too much or they promise to send personalized connection requests and then get lazy. Their metrics fall off considerably and they wonder what happened. They assume LinkedIn changed something.

LinkedIn does pay attention to how many connection requests are sent, how many are personalized, and how many are accepted. If the ratio is out of whack, they will send a warning. If the warning is not heeded, you can find yourself unable to send new connection requests.

I have seen this happen a handful of times in the last couple of months. It takes hours to withdraw all those unaccepted connection requests.

The time would have been far better spent personalizing and creating value by standing out with a good message.

Consider who you remember after meeting or talking with someone. It certainly wasn't the person who said nothing.

There are several things that I deem a best practice and personalizing your messaging is among the top.

Say A Few Words

Why do I want you to personalize your posts?

Really, it's the same reason. People are posting on LinkedIn more than ever so your Homepage feed moves quickly. When you introduce your post, the goal should be to pull people in to your post and have them click, like, comment, or share what you've created or shared.

Ask a question, add a couple of relevant hashtags, mention people and companies. Once again, in conversation, you wouldn't mention a podcast, article, or book without telling people why they should watch, listen, or read it.

Realize that on the other side of the screen and across the keyboard is another human being. That person can potentially help you advance your business or career.

TAKEAWAY

If someone can make a difference in your career or business (which could be almost everyone), they deserve a proper introduction to you.

ACTION

Set a goal to increase the amount you personalize on LinkedIn and other places.

Show up like you care.

TIP

It's hard to be impressed with someone if you don't know why you should be.

OBSERVATION

More and more, people are less likely to connect with people they don't know.

CHAPTER 12

Before You Automate, Pause and Consider

Between emails, InMails, and connection requests, I receive a weekly stream of questions about automating LinkedIn outreach. Over the years, I heard hundreds of stories of how people have used LinkedIn successfully and how others have failed miserably at achieving the results they desired. People have sent me their favorite app, tool, or method ranging from a Chrome extension to a customized tool they created.

My response to people and their emails is the same. "If someone's business is worth $1,000, $10,000, $100,000 or $1,000,000, don't they deserve a personalized approach? Would you really expect a buyer to want to respond or engage with you from a generic connection request or message?

If it's coming from the company or organization, that's a different situation. That's marketing.

I believe that sales is a 1:1 engagement and that marketing is 1:many. Using automation for business development and sales is an attempt to make a 1:1 experience a 1:many experience. I am not saying every message or introduction needs to be 100% customized. I do mean that the message you send must resonate with the person receiving said message.

In the short term, automation may work. In the long run, not so much.

The person may not be interested. However, they understand why they received the message in the first place.

At any given time, I have a number of connection requests from people I don't know who are absolutely sure they can help me increase Intero's lead generation efforts and results. I always wonder if they've looked at my profile. Probably not. Otherwise they'd know that I'm not a likely prospect.

> Hi Colleen!
>
> I just came across Intero Advisory searching through and I was very impressed with all of the outstanding work! Is Intero Advisory interested in finding more clients right now?
>
> Here at ⬛⬛⬛⬛, we help B2B companies just like yours leverage Linkedin and other social platforms to generate at least 20 high-quality business and sales opportunities every month.
>
> If you're looking to scale predictably, and fill your sales pipelines with new, targeted, and well-qualified leads - then when are you available over the next few days for a call with me?
>
> I have some ideas that I'd love to share with you!

As a Vistage Speaker, I have Vistage in the Experience section of my LinkedIn profile. I receive connection requests and messages from other speakers suggesting they would like to connect and be a speaker for my Vistage group. I do not lead a Vistage group. It's not my profile that is confusing. The automation they use picks me up from particular keywords they've chosen as important which are on my profile.

Knowing how to leverage LinkedIn for business development is a significant part of our service offerings.

We stay current on automation tools and ensure we make recommendations that increase the effectiveness of our client's LinkedIn strategy. However, reviewing and testing LinkedIn automation apps and software could be a full-time job.

When it comes to LinkedIn outreach, automated tools are NOT among our recommendations.

If you automate or are planning to automate your LinkedIn outreach, please read on.

Few teams spend time actually hand-selecting LinkedIn profiles for clients. Our team is one of those few. In 2020, we've sourced more than 60,000 C-level profiles. Between 2018 and 2020, that number was over 130,000.

The operative word is hand-selected. Is it slower, more complicated?

Yes.

It also yields better results.

Why?

Automation presumes that LinkedIn's searches are always correct and that LinkedIn members add their information correctly to their profile.

Flawed assumptions.

How do I know these are not reasonable assumptions?

We see it firsthand.

Not too long ago, a client of ours was about to onboard a new client. The client had somewhere between $15K and $90K in potential lifetime value and was lost because one of their colleagues was using automation and reached out to the same prospect. In the end, no one closed the business.

Often clients come to us after they've hired an outsourced LinkedIn lead generator or subscribed to an automation tool. Before we can implement our process, we have to clean out their networks and withdraw pending requests to people who probably saw the invitation and wonder why it came their way.

Here are two examples of invitations that went to an intended CEO or President. The first example was sent to a young woman who is a student. The automation picked up that she was a "president." She was, of her sorority.

The second example clearly shows that the message was sent to someone who is a color analyst. Somewhere on this profile, he had "president" or "CEO."

The automation picked up the right word and profile but was unable to see it was not the right context.

While you may say that's only two examples, we see this occur over and over again.

We are not against ALL automation. In full disclosure, we use Dux Soup (an automation tool). However, we never use it for visiting profiles, sourcing, or outreach. We strictly use it to minimize time spent on creating spreadsheets manually.

I have spoken with some of the developers of these automated tools and they recognize the pitfalls. They focus on quantity over quality.

If we thought you could use automation successfully in LinkedIn we would be all for it. However, time and time again we see all the ways the results go wonky really fast.

Outsmarting LinkedIn?

LinkedIn and Microsoft have some of the most talented people in the world on their teams. That is NOT to say that others aren't equally talented. However, most of the creators of the automated tools I've seen don't have the resources to compete with LinkedIn and Microsoft.

It's similar to trying to outsmart Google. It's a futile attempt.

Google "LinkedIn lead generation software, tools or extensions" and notice the large number of results for this search. Depending on how you search, this number varies greatly.

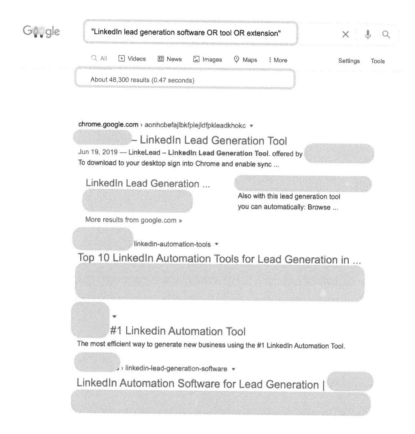

There is also another type of automation where fake accounts are created for business development. While this may not be as well known or promoted as directly as automation tools, it exists.

This approach, depending on who you are and what you do, may create an even more detrimental impression.

Automation is pretty clear so if someone responds to an automated message they typically know they are. If they do, it may mean they are in a ready state to buy. That's good if you're the one sending the message.

A fake profile where you're setting up someone as real who is not is different. This is my impression. To me, it feels shamelessly spammy. More disingenuous and more like you are trying to fool others.

If business development and sales are the engine's fuel, shouldn't the strategy and implementation be of the highest integrity?

Caveat emptor
You may want to review their claims regarding their success rates and their transparency about the data.

You use automation to increase the number of people you want to reach and make it easier on yourself. So, it's all about you?

You may want to Google "customer journey" or "voice of the customer."

Have you considered how you'll come across to the person you want to talk to and buy from you? Do you even care?

Connections are people
Throughout this book, I've referenced the importance of people, of genuinely connecting with and talking to people.

I don't believe that most people in the B2B world want to buy from bots or automated messages. They want to know there is a real person on the other side of the exchange. Today more than ever, people want to minimize risk as much as possible and so they want to buy, recommend, and refer to what they know is REAL.

If you don't care, then automation is right for you. If, on the other hand, you consider the other people worth knowing, then automating your LinkedIn outreach will feel cringe-worthy.

LinkedIn pays attention to your network and its relevance. The more relevant your network, the better for you. Build a good network, a good community of professionals, and you position yourself to create opportunity.

Not interested in building a relevant network, just interested in profiles that may or may not be your ideal client or prospect? Go for the automation and consider it the equivalent of the Yellow Pages.

Remember the Yellow Pages?

It's always the process

An organized and transparent process that considers how LinkedIn works and how most people fill out their profile is the key to better results.

Our best clients trust the process.

They understand why we include the steps we do and what we're looking for before reaching out.

It doesn't work for everyone, and, in the end, it's about the person, their offering, and the value they create.

LinkedIn lead generation is more than a numbers game. It's your entree to be known, respected, and worthy of someone's business.

TAKEAWAY

Each outreach, from the first one, creates an impression of you.

 ACTION

If you are using automation, review specific numbers, e.g., connection acceptance rate, people who express an interest in talking with you, new meetings/calls and closed business.

The same applies for anyone in a job search. Closed business might relate to job offers extended to you.

 TIP

The numbers that we track on behalf of our clients support that automation is not as effective as a personalized, hand-selected process.

 OBSERVATION

Anyone who can hire you as an employee, service or solution provider should warrant a more personalized outreach than what an automated tool can provide.

CHAPTER 13

How Do You Measure Social Influence?

STANDOUT

Focus on quantifiable business and career results, not impressions, views, and likes.

Social influence is an interesting topic. It seems that we've added the word "social" to the front of several words and they've taken on a new and more relevant meaning. Think social media, social selling, and social influence. Sometimes I find myself in that quintessential Golden Retriever head tilt and wonder what these phrases actually mean.

I'm not trying to be flippant. However, I do want to understand what people want when they refer to social influence.

Influence

Dr. Robert Cialdini has been referred to as the most often quoted living psychologist, best known for his seminal 1984 book on persuasion and marketing titled *Influence: The Psychology of Persuasion,* and his findings on social proof are particularly relevant to elevating your online presence and reputation. When you combine and leverage several of these "weapons of influence" you have a greater chance of being seen, recognized, and approached.

My friend and fellow Vistage speaker Dean Minuto is Cialdini trained and an expert in this area.

Dean's talk, YESCALATE® GET TO YES FASTER® has been heard more than 900 times within the Vistage community and presented to tens of thousands of CEOs and leaders—and he received the Vistage Speaker of the Year Award in 2015.

When I asked Dean about social influence during an interview in mid-2020, we talked about how our brains work—because the brain uses shortcuts to make decisions. And if we can uncover those invisible shortcuts, we can put them to work for us in an honest and ethical way—actually helping people make decisions (hence the subtitle of his Talk, GET TO YES FASTER®).

The brain is predictable and it LIKES predictable—it likes patterns because patterns are safe. Meaning that people feel less at risk when they see those patterns. Influence begins in the small things and patterns that people can see in their environment. Those things can attract or repel us. Scientists refer to these patterns of decision making, these shortcuts as "cognitive biases." If you were to look up that term in Wikipedia, you would see that there are more than 188 of them. Dean summarizes them as seven key points in a model he developed and calls MAGNETS™ because they can help us attract a yes and get a yes to stick. He outlines them in his book, *The One-Page Sales Coach*. They include:

M for Motion:
The bias is to consistency and a thing in motion stays in motion.

A for Ask:
This is called framing or perceptual contrast—and we create it with questions.

G for Give:
We feel pressure (a bias) to give back when we are given something.

N for Nice:
We are biased to relate to people we like—and those who
are like us. AND those who *like* us.

E for Evidence:
People look for proof of what others have already chosen.

T for Trust:
Packaging (uniforms) and endorsements (diplomas) provide
a shortcut.

S for Supply:
The forcing mechanism of deadlines and limited numbers.

Clearly what you do matters. And if you are conscious of these shortcuts you can be intentional about using them to make more of a
difference in the world.

Dean's model is the quintessential blueprint for building influence.
I encourage you to explore and study his work to increase your credibility and ability to advance your business and career. Check out
his website at yescalate.com.

Here is an example of how to weave several of these shortcuts into
major influence by using the Give and the Nice components in
Dean's model.

Two activities you can complete today are to go on LinkedIn and:

1. Give a recommendation
2. Make an introduction between two of your contacts who
   would benefit from being connected. What a gift and how
   nice of you!

**Give a recommendation and introduce others by answering
these three questions:**

1. What is the problem that person solved for you? Dean notes
   that the first thing people think about is THEMSELVES

because the brain is wired to SURVIVE so be specific as to how you think that relates to them.

2. How are they different from someone else who could have solved that same problem? This recommendation is also rooted in brain science as Dean notes that people pay attention to anything that is DIFFERENT.

3. How would you describe them to someone who doesn't know them or hasn't worked with them before? As Dean has pointed out, there are only FIVE ways to get something into someone's brain—the five senses—and one of those is the king: visual processing. Help people see this person the way you do.

These may be two of the most valuable activities you complete today: give a recommendation and make an introduction.

 TAKEAWAY

Decide what you want to achieve when you're on LinkedIn. Influence and respect are built over time.

 ACTION

Think about who influences you and why.

Who do you emulate in your industry and why?

What can you do to create or enhance your level of influence?

 TIP

Ask others the questions listed and pay attention to their answers.

 OBSERVATION

Being loud is different than being influential. Choose influential.

CHAPTER 14

Don't Believe Your Own Press

STANDOUT

Generate long-term social capital for yourself and your career.

Building your business is more important than all the likes and shares.

Peaking too early or too quickly usually poses more issues than not. It typically takes years to gain the expertise you need to stand out and be known. While it's different now because of social media and the biggest stars on Instagram, YouTube, and TikTok may have millions of followers and advertisers, we're once again not talking about that.

LinkedIn is different. You should want to differentiate yourself so that you can advance your business and career. That is a goal worth aspiring to.

I am continually reminded of the sheer grit it takes to build a reputation, build a community, and be recognized among your peers, team, and industry as a leader of one or many.

Careers are made and businesses grow when people know who you are. When you've established gravitas you don't need to find or buy connections or followers. You attract people by virtue of the value you create for others through your purpose, work, or mission.

The majority of CEOs, founders, and executive leaders are not household names and aren't making news every day. Most days they are working on or in their business and that means endless initiatives, meetings, rah-rahing, fundraising, reporting, and selling. These leaders are tuned in to their place in the world, how vital their contributions are, and the responsibility they shoulder.

They are confident and humble, poised and ready to help, here to serve rather than be served.

Others share way too much about themselves and they share their stories repeatedly.

They do get engagement. Lots of views, likes, and comments.

The engagement feeds their ego and they believe they are building a platform.

They share more and their network reacts more.

You might ask, "Isn't that the idea?"

Yes and no.

Yes, you want engagement. You also want conversion.

No, because often engagement doesn't lead to conversion. Most decision makers and buyers aren't spending time engaging with your content. They're not that into you.

When I have more than a ten-minute conversation with them, I often learn what's missing in their equation. **Real engagement leads to relationships that increase revenue and/or career opportunities.**

Revenue or Likes

I will forsake engagement in the way of likes, comments, and shares for cultivating relationships that generate revenue and valued relationships.

I don't know about you but I've never figured out how to take all those likes, reactions, comments, and shares to the bank.

For those who don't need to concern themselves with revenue, go for it.

Most people that I know in business are there to build their business, feed their family, and build a career that opens doors and provides new opportunities.

If that's you, don't believe your own press.

Never assume that what made you successful indicates your future success. We are in uber-rapid change and disruption.

We're all a bit exhausted by the talkers and promoters. Let the doers, makers, and workers prevail.

Build your personal brand with a dose of humility, a sense of humor, and a genuine understanding of who you are and you will attract people to you.

As I write this, I am reminded of an email I read this week from someone who has rebranded themself and their business and basically shouted throughout the email that they didn't really ever like what they were doing before. They didn't like how they had branded themselves.

Please note they were not talking about their colors, style guide, website, and email template. They were talking about the core of their business offering and the issues and topics they attached themselves to for a number of years.

I'm not disputing the idea of changing your business. Have at it. Sometimes it's vital and needed.

However, I was struck by how boldly they rejected all they had stood for. I have thought about it for days. I'm not sure about others but I know I would be disappointed and might even feel a bit taken if I was a client who had invested in what they had offered.

You can only serve so many people in a given day, week, month, year, decade, and career. You need to choose who you serve.

If you choose to serve your clients, you will probably gain more credibility and build your business.

If you choose to serve your followers, your groupies, and your likers, you may end up feeding your ego more than your bank account.

The CEOs and business owners I know and have had the privilege to work with understand how to navigate this and choose their clients first, always.

TAKEAWAY

Remember where you started and how your career and business grew and changed.

 ACTION

Ask yourself if you sound authentic, confident, and open-minded or if your tone could be viewed as pompous, self-righteous, and arrogant.

Close your eyes and consider how you would respond to you.

 TIP

Never underestimate the power of words and the impression you make, positive or negative.

 OBSERVATION

Let your actions and credentials speak for you.

CHAPTER 15

Getting to Know Someone

STANDOUT

Build your reputation by taking the time to develop strategic relationships.

Speed networking has been off my radar for a while now. It's just not enough anymore. The five to ten minutes of uber-high level pleasantries, quick questions focused on what you do, who you know, and why you're there just don't cut it anymore. These brief conversations are meant to foster quick hits, new introductions, and potentially a follow-up, not an in-depth conversation that creates a meaningful connection and potential relationship.

I've noticed this for a while. When I step back and give it some thought, I realize that I've paused only a particular kind of networking. In fact, most of my days, weeks, months, and years add up to one enormous, powerful networking event.

The best networking I do is when I have the opportunity to spend two or three hours with a group of open-minded people who seek to grow their businesses and themselves through continually learning ways to think about their businesses and careers. I am privileged to work with CEOs and senior leaders through Vistage, TAB, LXCouncil, EO, and other organizations. It is through these and other focused exchanges that we spark new connections.

I gave up rapid-fire coffee meetings long ago since they quickly became "pick your brain" sessions. If you look carefully, you can see my entire body cringe when someone asks if they can "pick my brain." The term is uninspired and sounds pretty nasty and invasive to me. I'm happy to provide a nugget or two. That's not the point. However, have a few of those in a week and you realize you're diminishing your worth.

Now I focus on a "less is more" approach. Some of my discovery calls and meetings are spent talking with people about their vision for themselves, their families, and their business, not how we can work together. I learn about their family, what makes them tick, how they've come to this place, why they do the work they do. The stories are fascinating. And, I find they are good with sharing as it provides the context if we eventually work together.

There is a resurgence, I believe, in actually knowing people. Knowing people is powerful. It connects you to a greater sense of community, intentionality, and purpose. It enables you to make a difference. I mentioned this earlier in the book. This is a good stride in the right direction and speaks to the opportunity even as we work remotely.

And, from what I hear when I talk with and interview others, helping others is what motivates them to do whatever it is they do. To help someone, you need first to know them.

Your call to action this week is to nurture a connection you've already met. Give them a ring, send them a text or message, and invite them to have a distraction-free conversation. And, then when you meet them, turn off your phone and enjoy getting to know someone with no agenda other than the one that brews up over being interested in someone else.

TAKEAWAY

Conversations, even initial ones, are different now. More real and interesting.

ACTION

If conversation making is not your thing, consider how you will appear to others and how you can rely on a couple of questions to ease into a conversation.

TIP

Getting to know people creates referral opportunities and introductions. It's worth the time it takes.

OBSERVATION

Don't fool yourself into thinking that real, authentic conversations and relationships can be replaced by AI, bots, or automation.

CHAPTER 16

Your Customers See You

STANDOUT

Others will vet you online. Ensure you make a favorable impression.

When online, where do your customers/clients/prospects spend time?

What's their platform of choice? Have you asked them?

If not, please do.

Over the years, the CEO, owner, or in-house marketing person has shared with me that their marketing agencies focused their marketing strategies on Facebook, not LinkedIn. When I asked why, the only answer they could come up with was because it's what the agency said and, "It's the largest social platform, right?"

There has to be a better and more complete answer than that, don't you think?

As they shared these stories, I'd jump over to Facebook and LinkedIn to see some of the numbers. It was interesting.

Company #1 had 328 more followers on LinkedIn than Facebook (difference of 208%), and yet the focus was on Facebook retargeting.

Company #2 had 340 more followers on LinkedIn than Facebook (a difference of 37%), and yet LinkedIn did not make it into the social marketing strategy.

One of our largest clients has 14,000 more followers on LinkedIn than Facebook (a difference of 54%) and their ideal clients are CEOs, CFOs, and COOs. While they focus on Facebook, their primary social channel for leads is LinkedIn. Based on feedback, Facebook is not among the channels that converts for them.

When I ask leaders where the traffic to their website comes from, few people can answer that question.

During a training session, a CEO raised his hand and said his marketing firm's content strategy focused on LinkedIn, but they saw no results so they stopped sharing content. When I asked him if he knew which social channel drove the most traffic to his website, he said he was sure it was Facebook.

A few minutes later he raised his hand and apologized for his oversight. He logged in to his Google Analytics and saw that LinkedIn sent more people to his website than any other social platform, and in this case, 78% of his website traffic originating on a social channel came from LinkedIn. In less than five minutes, he saw the data. Look for the data.

Everyone thinks Facebook is the golden child. For some, it is.

Facebook has always been personal: friends and family first. Businesses interrupt the flow on Facebook. On LinkedIn, it's all business and it's where you belong.

LinkedIn's role in B2B marketing has gained traction. The numbers demonstrate LinkedIn may be Cinderella and not the stepsister, after all.

We primarily work with CEOs and leadership. Typically they are the first to say they aren't on social media and not on Facebook in particular.

As one of our interns mentioned in a meeting the other day, "Why would they be on Facebook during the day or in the evening looking at other businesses?" Interesting question from a college senior who vets every brand and typically follows the CEO on Instagram or LinkedIn before buying anything.

It's important to ask questions and understand where your customers are. It's important to ask your customers and not just rely on your agency, no matter how good they are. If the social media person running your account is well versed on Facebook and not LinkedIn, do you think they are going to be able to advise objectively and accurately?

Ask your CFO if they make decisions about your vendors from what they see on Facebook. Ask your peers how they make their buying decisions. Think about how you make your decisions.

TAKEAWAY

Invest in places where your primary audience (recruiters, prospects, and clients) spend time. If they don't spend time or find value in a particular platform, reconsider why you're there.

ACTION

Evaluate where you are and what the return is for being there.

TIP

Don't assume that anything works. Ask for the data to verify that you're investing in the right platforms and strategies.

OBSERVATION

Review this on a quarterly basis in case something changes.

CHAPTER 17

All Selling (Hmm, Influence) is Social

STANDOUT

Distinguish yourself by developing your skills, value proposition, and network.

Let me just say it. I am not a fan of the term social selling. I resisted the term and am relieved it has lost its buzzword status of late.

When people asked me if we taught social selling I'd immediately ask them what they meant by the term. The range of answers was off the charts.

They typically wanted to learn how to use social media to drive leads. Not a bad idea. However, they often had a sales team that was not interested in learning anything about social media. The road to social selling is riddled with obstacles and lack of understanding.

For quite some time, we led with the idea that selling has always been social rather than promote the term.

The term social selling gained increasing popularity when LinkedIn launched Sales Navigator in July of 2014.

With more than 30 years of sales experience, everything I've ever learned and experienced as a sales professional has related to refining my ability to engage with people, establish an exchange of value, and build relationships.

Social selling is the process of developing relationships as part of the sales process. Today this often takes place via LinkedIn and social networks.

Examples of social selling techniques include sharing relevant content, interacting directly with potential buyers and customers, personal branding, and social listening. Social selling is gaining popularity in a variety of industries.

Koka Sexton, Founder, Koka Sexton Consulting and a LinkedIn alum, put it this way: "The ultimate goal of adopting social networks as part of your sales process is to build stronger relationships with your buyers. Visibility creates opportunity and leveraging those opportunities to build a stronger connection with the decision makers in your network will pay huge dividends over time."

Social Selling is More Than a Buzzword

While social selling is sometimes confused with social marketing, there are two key differences. First, social selling is focused on sales professionals rather than marketing professionals. Second, social selling aims to cultivate one-on-one relationships, rather than broadcast one-to-many messages.

Why?

Let's take a look at what social selling entails.

Sharing Relevant Content

Which content is relevant and valuable is subjective.

Yes, that's true. The most relevant content is original content created by you or your organization.

Oh, you're not creating any content. How about industry content? Could you curate content from your industry association?

"Well, I could curate content but I think it will mention several of our competitors since they create their own content, they have videos and case studies and the association picks up their stuff and they get quoted a lot because of that. Is the content relevant if it includes information about my competitors?"

It's relevant for them and I'm sure they'd be thrilled that you share it. However, it's not relevant for you.

Interacting Directly with Potential Buyers and Customers

"Someone just connected with me. What do I do now?"

Send them a quick message and say, "Great to connect, thanks." Let them know you're always open to a conversation. Keep it simple.

"That seems so odd."

Why? If you met at an event or in their office and they introduced themselves you would say, "Good to meet you," or "Thanks for saying hello."

"Then what?"

Interact, engage. Can you send them a recent blog post, case study, video, invite to a webinar that may be interesting to them? Know what they might find valuable. Oh wait, that's right, you don't have any content. How about finding some from someone else other than a competitor?

The Wall Street Journal, Fast Company, Inc., and LinkedIn are great places to find content!

Personal Branding

"I'm a private person. I'm not on Facebook. I don't get this personal branding thing."

You can be a private person, still look good on LinkedIn and be relevant in the digital world.

"Yeah, but, uh, I mean, I'm better in person and I don't need that online stuff. My clients know me and I'm not that big on finding new customers anyway. Just not my thing."

Oh, I see. So if I could show you how you could connect with your customers online and learn more about them and see who they know, that's not of interest? And, I can show you how to find more of those customers. Would that be helpful to your company if not to you?

"Yes, but..."

When I hear, "Yes but," I know we have a mindset issue and this conversation is going one place: downhill.

Writing this in late 2020 is interesting. It's the first time I've heard less pushback and I think that's due to the fact that up until early March, business deals had been flowing pretty well even for those who didn't do any of what we as LinkedIn trainers and coaches advocate.

It's a new day. There aren't a lot of options now. In person, if it's happening, is curtailed and for many of us, me included, just not worth the risk.

Social Listening

"What? Isn't social listening an oxymoron?"

Good question. It refers to listening that takes place online. Yes, you can call it reading. It's about understanding what people are saying online in their posts, comments, and reactions.

On LinkedIn it's a way to see what colleagues, competitors, etc., are talking about. Show your knowledge in your particular area of expertise.

"Hmm. Not sure about that. Can I just like it? That seems safe."

At this point in the conversation, I simply say, "Sure."

Leaders: Is this kind of conversation happening among your sales team? If so, you need to fix it. I suggest you begin with what you're doing personally.

This social selling thing is not so simple.
Some sales professionals are excellent at it. They get it and are off engaging with people and making hay. For others, it's difficult and discouraging.

Mostly, we find that people don't want to make an error, get in trouble, or look foolish.

As it relates to content on LinkedIn, please be careful to respect that it's a professional network and is not a place for too many personal posts (one every once in a while is fine), politics, or religion unless that is your professional area. There's no need to unknowingly annoy someone you could work with or for because you've used a particular network incorrectly.

For most people though, there is nothing to worry about. You're not going to go rogue.

If in doubt, leaders, give your employees some guidance. It will make a difference.

Few people still use the phrase social selling. It's a bit dated now.

I'd rather call it selling in a social world. That is what it is. There's no going back.

When a CEO, president, or owner calls or emails and wants to know about our social selling program, it's a good indicator they just read a book, watched something on YouTube, or heard a presentation from a sales trainer and social selling was mentioned more than once.

In theory, the right idea. However, just think about selling smart in a new economy—an economy reeling from and coming to terms with a pandemic.

Selling is a relationship-building process.
Each step along the process must create trust, credibility, and insight.

The person you're interacting with must see immediate value and see that you are who you say you are. There is no way around that. Trying to jump over the touchpoints that someone needs to understand before they can engage with you lessens your opportunity and adds to the time they need to decide.

Leads or opportunities must come from a variety of sources. Your marketing team will run email campaigns, your content strategy (video, blogs, case studies, white papers, webinars, podcasts, events), SEO, and website development. Usually the goal is to reach a larger audience and gain awareness.

Yes, of course, some content will be created for your middle and bottom of the sales funnel audience and buyers.

When your salespeople take your content and send it to or share it with their prospects and customers along with their personalized take on the content, they are positioning themselves to spark a conversation.

Few sales or engagements occur in B2B without people talking.

You and your salespeople, customer service and marketing people need to be comfortable talking to people online and knowing how to turn that into a phone call, Zoom meeting, or at some point, a face-to-face meeting.

We find that most people think a quick question via email or through direct messaging is their chance to sell.

It's not unless the person asking questions or commenting tells you they are interested in buying immediately.

Otherwise, create an opportunity to talk then listen and ask good questions.

If you're not interested in this method and only want to automate the process, you will need to reach a lot of people and will probably have a lower conversion rate.

Kevin McKeown, a Master Chair for Vistage Worldwide and client of ours, always says, "We're looking for people in a ready state and the sooner they hear your voice, the better."

Finding people in a ready state is not something they will have on their LinkedIn profile or any social profile. They may post that they are looking for something or someone but posts are fleeting. They need to be tagged with relevant hashtags or shared with you. Otherwise, you might not find it.

So, finding people in a ready state means reaching a larger number of people, catching the eye and attention of people who are curious and potentially interested and let them reach out to you.

At that point they will most likely have vetted you on Google and LinkedIn to make sure you are the person you say you are.

Additionally, do they have enough context to understand who you are and what you do? If not, that's a missed opportunity for you. And that's on you.

Is what Kevin talks about relevant? Yes.

By building his personal brand online, meaning strategically and continually developing content on his website, LinkedIn, and social channels, Kevin is positioning himself as an expert and leader.

Combining his personal brand with nurturing and expanding his professional network of C-level leaders and leveraging the brand of a worldwide organization builds a solid foundation and platform for driving results.

Kevin McKeown is all about results.

You may get lucky and gain online traction quickly. If so, that's great but it's a loud and noisy place. For most people, it doesn't work that way. You need a runway and how long that runway is will be determined by how strong your brand and credibility is, how strong your network is, and how you take interest in engaging with others. The more those are all lined up and working on your behalf, the better.

TAKEAWAY

There are new ways to connect and develop relationships. However, selling remains the same.

ACTION

Know where your prospects and clients are.

Interact with them where they show up.

Create context and value for you and your business.

TIP

Strive to always be at the top of your profession by continually honing your skills, method, and experiences.

OBSERVATION

People want to buy. They just don't want to be sold.

Stand out and be different.

CHAPTER 18

Ghosting Goes Both Ways in Recruiting and Sales

STANDOUT

Never compromise your value by accepting less than professional behavior.

Ghosting, while a popular term these days, is nothing new, and there's not a day that goes by that an article on ghosting doesn't appear in one or more of my feeds. Mostly, the articles refer to recruiting and extend to both the candidate and the employer.

People within companies have ghosted people for decades. It was a common and accepted practice. Hiring managers, buyers, and executives have considered it regular practice to not acknowledge a sales inquiry or job application or respond to a person's request for an interview. Perhaps they had a hiring and sales inquiry process but most companies don't. So why don't they respond?

Between 2016 and the first quarter of 2020, the tables turned and the candidate was sought after. When they didn't show up for an interview, everyone was shocked and dissing the person who didn't show up. I am not condoning this behavior. However, it's curious to me that people within the company didn't see it coming. People in some cities and professions were responding to multiple inquiries and even offers.

Let me repeat that. I am not condoning bad behavior. It takes minutes to leave a voicemail, send an email, or text.

It's important to respect everyone's time and interest. Be civil and respond quickly, especially when you're the one who is seeking a new employee. How you treat them before and during the interview process speaks volumes. It reflects your culture and your communication skills.

Sales ghosting

Anyone who has spent any time in sales has experienced the prospect "going dark." It's part of any sales process.

There is no more difficult job than that of the business development and sales professionals within your company.

It always struck me as odd when CEOs and business owners tell me they can't stand all the sales calls and yet they expect their salespeople to make similar calls and connections. Huh?

We all need to remember that developing and closing new business and expanding current business is essential, no, critical. Now more than ever, these sales people are the bridge to new ideas, products, and services that you may not even know you need but you actually do given the changes we have all experienced in 2020.

Do I think all sales professionals do a great job? No, I don't. It's critical for a sales professional to be a perpetual student, always curious, and focused on their customer/client.

According to Spotio, only 39% of people intended to go into sales.

Training and coaching is essential, especially if you're hiring the 61% that just happened into sales.

I remember choosing to go into sales. I couldn't imagine a better job and career. I still feel that way.

Sales professionals need to think about the missed opportunities that slip through their fingers every day. If they do that, will there be less ghosting? Perhaps. The statistics indicate that this may be true.

Consider:

- 73% of executives prefer to work with sales professionals referred by someone they know. (Source: International Data Corporation [IDC])

- Salespeople who actively seek out and leverage referrals earn 4 to 5 times more than those who don't. (Brevit)

- 84% of buyers now kick off their buying process with a referral. (Harvard Business Review)

- 92% of buyers trust referrals from people they know. (Nielsen)

- 91% of customers say they'd give referrals. Only 11% of salespeople ask for referrals. (Dale Carnegie)

- 84% of B2B decision makers begin their buying process with a referral, according to the Sales Benchmark Index.

Worse than ghosting someone you don't know is ghosting someone that you've been referred or introduced to. Salespeople, candidates, and employers all deserve better.

TAKEAWAY

Ghosting is not new. With great transparency, people know more about you, good and bad.

ACTION

Be clear about next steps and either respond or set the expectation that you may not be able to respond to every inquiry.

TIP

Try not to be the person ghosting others. Text messages and emails take seconds to send.

OBSERVATION

The people who realize the human side of business tend to take a moment and think about the potential unintended consequences.

CHAPTER 19

Every Referral is an Opportunity

STANDOUT

*Always identify, connect, and know
the best talent in your industry.*

For the last four years, recruiting has been at the forefront of every call, meeting, or workshop with leaders across the country. I ended March 11, 2020 thinking we were starting the following week with four new recruiting projects. On March 12, I learned that those projects were put on hold.

Since March, we've all witnessed either personally, throughout networks or in the media, an unprecedented number of people seeking new opportunities.

As I reread and edited this chapter ahead of moving into book production, I was reminded that earlier in the day, I read in the *Wall Street Journal* that four companies were laying significant numbers of people off: Disney is laying off 28,000, Allstate is laying off 8,000, United Airlines and American Airlines are laying off 32,000. That is 68,000 people among four companies.

Another *Wall Street Journal* article, "Is It Insane to Start a Business During Coronavirus? Millions of Americans Don't Think So," dated September 26, 2020, reported that applications for the employer identification numbers that entrepreneurs need to start a business have passed 3.2 million so far this year, compared with 2.7 million at the same point in 2019, according to the U.S. Census Bureau. That group includes gig-economy workers and other independent contractors who may have struck out on their own after being laid off.

Even excluding those applicants, new filings among a subset of business owners who tend to employ other workers reached 1.1 million through mid-September, a 12% increase over the same period last year and the most since 2007, the data shows.

Of course, other companies are growing and hiring. Not everyone though will benefit or be able to transfer their skills.

Recruiting will come back. There is no doubt. That's why it's important to cover this topic. Be prepared for your next hiring wave.

Create a talent bench by at least connecting with others who might be potential candidates at some point. Get to know the world-class contributors and emerging and current leaders in your industry.

Don't be caught with a lightweight talent pipeline. I asked Jim Cusick, our Director of Digital Enablement, to share the insight he provides our clients. Think about how you can elevate your talent and recruiting process after reading what Jim has to say.

Jim's thoughts on recruiting

"Acquiring the right talent is the most important key to growth. Hiring was—and still is—the most important thing we do."

This quote by Salesforce founder Marc Benioff emphasizes the importance of finding the right people. Recruiting the right people is not easy and there is some luck involved. However, with the right methodical approach, you can be successful.

Timing is the variable. It needs to be suitable for the candidate, the company, the team, and sometimes the referral. When the stars align and you make the right decision, the business can reap the benefits of the investment for years to come.

The financial commitment for recruiting can range from a few hundred dollars for a job ad or thousands of dollars for a placement fee to full competitive salaries of an internal recruiting team. Depending on the type of business, any of these investments could be the right fit. It's important to remember that any investment pays off when you bring the right people into the organization.

The majority of companies struggle with developing a multi-faceted strategic approach to attracting the right individuals to join their teams and improve overall performance. Typically, hiring is tasked to a manager but supported by Human Resources or Operations. This relationship creates reactionary and passive hiring strategies that can be time consuming.

Recruiting has evolved with the introduction of data analytics, artificial intelligence, and the gig economy. Businesses have had to alter their approach to bringing in top talent and leverage as many different channels as possible. Both the company and the job seeker must adapt to this new hiring landscape.

When you break it down to its simplest form, hiring still amounts to human interaction and **trust**.

The hiring manager must consider this question: With only limited interactions, do I believe that adding this candidate to our team will improve our business?

Job seekers need to look at it this way: based on the interviews and research, would this opportunity be a good fit?

What has changed is how we get to this simple human interaction. The bottom line is that no matter how effective technology becomes, there will be mistakes, miscommunication, and some reliance on luck. The goal is to leverage data and technology to ensure the best fit for everyone and mitigate poor hiring decisions.

The Best Time to Hire

There are many barriers to making a good hire. A half-hearted approach creates issues for all and makes it a less than enjoyable process. Before you even start the hiring process, you have to ask yourself, "Are you ready to hire?"

It can't be overstated that timing is everything. Starting a search without having all of the necessary information and processes in place could sabotage your efforts and drain your budget.

All too often, we see companies wait too long to start a search. Or, they launch a search ill-prepared. Both scenarios can cause issues and frustration. Too late indicates that they're so bogged down with work that they couldn't prepare. Too soon means that they haven't given the proper thought and strategy to a big decision.

Finding that "just right" time is tough. We can't fix an organization's challenges with bandwidth or lack of preparation. We say that you should always be pipelining. Keep making great connections in your industry and in the fields where you need new hires. When it comes time to bring someone on, you'll know exactly where to go first.

Branding

Another primary consideration before you hire is branding. You have to approach hiring in the same way as selling your product. Potential customers will research your company and job candidates will do the same thing. There needs to be a strategy around what they see and the information shared because it will influence whether someone decides to interview with you and most certainly it will influence whether they choose to join your organization.

If you're reaching out via LinkedIn, make sure that you have a LinkedIn company page with well-crafted messaging about your culture, your values, and your team initiatives. It should be consistent with your website and anywhere else that is easily searchable online.

It is also wise to take things a step further and have your existing employees advocate for the organization. Give them the tools to develop intentional LinkedIn profiles and website bios. Encourage them to share job posts and content related to your culture with their networks. Referrals are almost always good hires.

Workforce Planning

Most of the time, if a hiring manager decides to look for a new employee, they need the employee *now*. Most companies say, "I needed this person yesterday!" Sound familiar? Not today, not in 3 months, but yesterday. This simple phrase puts pressure on your candidate search and can quickly lead to issues. It can put your business in a bind on the recruiting they can do or cause a company to make the wrong hire. The chain reaction of being rushed to find someone immediately will inevitably impact the quality of the employment, the candidate experience, or lead you to attract candidates who are not the best fit.

Workforce planning cannot be fully automated (even though people are trying). However, insights from analytics should be involved in how you plan. Workforce planning needs to be a part of how you plan out a quarter, year, or 5-year roadmap.

While most companies say that their people are the most critical pieces of their organization, most don't devote enough attention to finding the right people. An organization should have a healthy fear of losing good employees. Losing employees is part of running a business and should be looked upon as such. You will be successful if you can initiate a proper exit plan, search mobilization, and a multi-channel approach toward recruiting potential candidates.

Good employees who leave can be a strong ally when it comes to attracting their replacement or future employees.

LinkedIn can quickly provide you with analytics that are necessary to create a proper workforce plan. You can search for:

- Salary information

- The number of candidates in your area who have the type of experience you require

- The number of candidates who are open to new opportunities

- The amount of similar open jobs in the area

- The types of people your competitors are hiring

There is no perfect solution or magic formula. However, if you have a workforce plan, you have a strategy. You can't predict when an employee will resign, have a personal emergency, or want a change of scenery. But you will be prepared. As Mike Tyson said, "Everyone has a plan until they get punched in the mouth." We would revise this for resource planning by saying, "Everyone thinks they have a plan until a great employee hands in their two weeks notice."

Measurable Hiring

What are the most important metrics for your recruiting and hiring process? If you have an immediate answer, you will most likely be on the right path to staying ahead of your competition in the war for talent. If you do not have an answer or are thinking, "How can I start using metrics to evaluate my process?" then you have some work to do.

We don't have to explain why metrics are essential. If you called your sales, finance, or operations leaders right now and asked them what their most important metrics are, they would be able to rattle them off immediately. These metrics ensure that those departments are successful. We see metrics absent from the hiring process because there is no standard process in place. Most approach hiring reactively, just hoping that the right candidate happens upon their recycled job description.

If you have metrics, you can accurately evaluate your processes to see what is and isn't working. The time, energy, and resources that companies spend on finding the right people to join their organization can be staggering. The only way to minimize these investments is by evaluating the process. LinkedIn has identified the metrics that will matter more as recruiting evolves: Quality of Hire, Sourcing Channel Effectiveness, and Assessment Effectiveness. If you would like to know more about how they chose these three, you can read the LinkedIn Talent Solutions e-Book titled *The Future of Recruiting*.

Once you have selected the metrics that make the most sense for your business, you need to confirm that you have a standardized hiring process. This process needs to be followed by everyone involved in recruiting and hiring. If the process is not standardized, you can't begin to use metrics to make informed business decisions. Over the next 6 to 12 months, be diligent about evaluating your process. Is it working? If the data points uncover specific bottlenecks or issues in the process, make those changes immediately. This way, you can start evaluating the changes in the process for their effectiveness.

In the beginning, you will need to experiment. Once you have a hiring process framework and metrics to evaluate your success, you will begin to see results. The goal is to efficiently build your candidate pipeline, reinforce the company brand in the job search marketplace, and bring the right people into your organization.

Recruiting With LinkedIn

LinkedIn is the most critical tool developed for recruiting. The platform provides more actionable data for both companies and individuals and it's free. LinkedIn has created a mini-economy that has drastically changed the recruiting landscape. Overnight LinkedIn minimized the gap between a "mom and pop" recruiting firm and an enterprise-level company with a recruiting call center. Everyone can now access the world's largest candidate pool.

LinkedIn took this a step further and created a premium tool called LinkedIn Recruiter. It provides all the features of a functional Applicant Tracking System (ATS) plus customer-facing candidate delivery functionality which is a game-changer.

LinkedIn Recruiter gives every recruiter, hiring manager, and HR professional the power to proactively find the right candidates for the role. The search filters allow you to get as granular as needed. The supporting features will help you craft the effective outreach to find qualified candidates. It is robust and there is a bit of a learning curve but it is designed to be intuitive.

Job Searching

Everyone who is an employee should be in a constant job search. Yes, you read that correctly. The keyword there is "employee." An employee is not a stakeholder in the company the way that a partner, owner, or family member is to the business. An employee, in this sense, is someone who has no ownership in the company.

There are varying degrees of a job search. The lowest degree is when you're happy with your current position and don't plan to leave but you have a strong online brand. You keep a running list of your achievements, contributions, and awards and keep them in one document. If the company were to go under, circumstances out of your control happen, or a perfect job opportunity falls into your lap, you're ready. The highest degree of a job search is when you are out of work and you need a job *now*.

LinkedIn estimates that up to 90% of people are open to the right opportunity. That is pretty much everyone.

We highly suggest that everyone who fits into the "employee" category should create a list of local companies of interest. You can do this by leveraging Glassdoor, networking and industry events, LinkedIn, and job postings. Glassdoor will give you a unique look into the company. Networking will not only help in your current role that you may never leave but give you insights into companies that you won't get online. Industry events are another place to network. They will also show you the innovators. LinkedIn will show you the brand, corporate values, and, most importantly, your potential future colleagues. Finally, job postings list technologies and job duties that outline the skills you need for the position. Active job seekers should complete this exercise as well but there is typically less emphasis on being picky.

If you are actively looking for a job and you are not on LinkedIn, you are practically swimming with weights in your hands. Can you do it? Yes. Are you going to be successful? Maybe. But there is an easier way. Why not put your best foot forward? Create an intentional professional profile. A strong LinkedIn profile will not only make it easy for proactive recruiting approaches to find you, but it will give the best first impression. The LinkedIn profile is your chance to stand out and drive your career forward. Additionally, you can customize your profile to show potential hiring managers or recruiters precisely what you are looking for to advance your career without notifying your current employer.

LinkedIn also has a tool for job seekers called Premium. With the Premium subscription, you receive analytics on competitors specifically for that position. Additionally, it gives you the ability to directly message the hiring managers, recruiters, or job posters to stand out from your competition. Premium subscribers find jobs two times faster than those who don't take advantage of this system.

LinkedIn gives job seekers leverage by arming them with the tools and data that would typically be cost-prohibitive. With this actionable data, everyone can make wiser career decisions.

Whether you are hiring, starting a business, or looking for a new role, LinkedIn offers tools to help you succeed. It comes down to old-fashioned person-to-person relationships and interactions. The tools on LinkedIn help you start the right conversations faster.

 TAKEAWAY

Recruiting, hiring, and onboarding is critical to your business success and requires a well thought out process.

 ACTION

Evaluate your current recruiting, hiring, and onboarding process and seek to understand what a candidate experiences.

 TIP

Hiring the people who will drive your organization forward and align with your values and mission makes all the difference.

 OBSERVATION

Become an ambassador to help everyone realize their career aspirations and you will build lifetime recruiting referrals.

CHAPTER 20

Spark That Conversation

STANDOUT

Generate business by creating value in every conversation.

Following on the theme of our last chapter, people are the opportunity.

Qualifying is a key step in the marketing, sales and recruiting process. However, for individuals though, opportunity extends beyond buying and recruiting. It's about learning more, gaining insight, networking, and career potential.

We also know the line between marketing and sales has blurred, and while that's a good thing in general, it does create role and accountability-morphing. When does real selling begin?

Think more strategically. Be creative and prepared.

I spoke with a potential client recently who straightaway said,

> *"I have received InMails, messages, and cold calls from lots of people just like you. I've never responded and the only reason we're talking is because you come highly recommended by a colleague."*

What could be better? I talked with a client today and we talked about this type of endorsement. It's every person's superpower, secret weapon. Developing a great network should be every salesperson's number one priority. Build the best network you can. Period.

And once you build this kick-ass network, make sure others are crystal clear about what you do. No one calls me and says: "I hear you're a social media expert." "I hear you specialize in Facebook, Twitter, Salesforce, Hubspot, AI, digital transformation." They do say, "I hear you specialize in LinkedIn." From there, I can elaborate.

While your business may be far more complex, your people (aka your professional network and ambassadors) should get it and be able to articulate who you are and what you do.

We've written extensively on the value of your network and your Centers of Influence. We believe they make a difference and the numbers reinforce this. Aja Frost, Head of Content SEO for Hubspot, shares insight on high-performing sales professionals in her article, "75 Key Sales Statistics That'll Help You Sell Smarter in 2020" which calls out the following:

- More than 40% of salespeople say prospecting is the most challenging part of the sales process, followed by closing (36%) and qualifying (22%).

- 84% of buyers now kick off their buying process with a referral.

- Nine in 10 buying decisions are made with peer recommendations.

- 92% of buyers trust referrals from people they know.

- After a positive experience, 83% of customers would be happy to provide a referral. But salespeople aren't asking: just 29% of customers end up giving a referral.

- 90% of buying decisions are made with peer recommendations.

If these numbers don't speak to you and show you a way to your sales pipeline, I'm not sure what will.

To every sales manager, there's one simple question: "How are you helping your salespeople build and leverage their professional relationships and network?"

What could be more important? Coach and encourage them to know the right people, whether they are inside or outside salespeople.

And guess what? When you need a new job, change careers, or enter a new phase of your career (and you will), many of the folks who care about you now and serve as your evangelists will help you again. Learn what works and deliver on it.

TAKEAWAY

Be clear about who you are, what your expertise is, and how you can support others in their initiatives.

ACTION

Stop pitching for a moment.

Have a conversation.

TIP

Never lose sight of the larger goal:

your business or career.

OBSERVATION

Building trust and credibility will always serve you well.

CHAPTER 21

The Economic Opportunity You Deserve

STANDOUT

Press on even in difficult circumstances and economies by increasing your own marketability.

In conversation, coaching, or training, I usually wrap up by saying, "We've covered a lot of ground today. We've talked about..." I summarize to remind people of key points, the ones I want them to reflect and initiate on.

I see the bigger picture, the better outcome, the possibility for each person to shape and influence their career or livelihood in a meaningful way. I see the opportunity for businesses, schools, nonprofits, and even governments to tell their own story with a view of the people who lead and work together.

Do you see this in your mind? If so, awesome! Now begin to bring it to life. This is your investment in you, your business and career.

If you've read, studied, skimmed, or passed this book on to a colleague, you've done more than most people do when they receive or purchase a book. Great work!

Make the most of your professional investment in yourself. Make time, act, don't give up, and respect the process of continuous improvement.

I consider it a success if you act on one nugget, start one conversation with someone new, or rethink your own strategy, personal bias, or hesitancy.

Your future opportunities are waiting for you.

Resources

Let's begin to shape your <u>individual</u> initiative.

Are you committed to being a STANDOUT?

Yes _____   No _____

Are you committed to taking the necessary time to elevate your online presence to advance your business and career initiatives?

Yes _____   No _____

If so, what will you commit to?

_____   I will build this out myself

_____   I will work with a trainer/coach/consultant to help me through the process

_____   I will hand this off to someone who will manage most of this for me

In order of importance, order the steps you need to take to advance your business and career initiative(s).

_____ I need to create, develop, or update my LinkedIn profile, resume, or bio

_____ I need to better develop, nurture, and expand my LinkedIn network

_____ I need to identify the Centers of influence, opportunities/ gaps in my network

_____ I need to create or enhance my activity on LinkedIn

_____ I need to work with a trainer/coach/consultant to help me

_____ I need to build or create my website

_____ I need to create original content

Custom priority _____

_____

When will you complete your most important action?

Date: _____

What will you consider a successful LinkedIn initiative?

_____

_____

Let's begin to shape your <u>company</u> initiative.

Are you committed to being a STANDOUT company?

Yes _____   No _____

Have you identified people within your company to serve as the champion or lead? This may be one person or a team and will typically include marketing, sales, human resources, and someone from the executive team.

Yes _____   No _____

Are elevating your corporate online presence, increasing employee presence and advocacy, and generating more business and recruiting opportunities part of your strategic plan?

Yes _____   No _____

If so, have you established corporate and individual KPIs for:

Marketing

Yes _____   No _____

   Company Page

   Yes _____ No _____

Sales

Yes _____   No _____

   Overall goals

   Yes _____ No _____

   Individual salespeople

   Yes _____ No _____

Human Resources

Yes _____   No _____

   Culture

   Yes _____ No _____

   Hiring/recruiting

   Yes _____ No _____

If not, how will you view it within your company's priority of initiatives?

_____

_____

Considering your budget, capacity, and individual resources, how will you proceed?

_____ We will build this out internally

_____ We will work with a trainer/coach/consultant to help us

_____ We will hand this off to a trainer/coach/consultant to manage for us

In order of importance, order the steps you need to take to advance your business and career initiative(s).

_____   We need to create, develop, or update LinkedIn
profiles for:

     _____   Leadership

      _____   _____

      _____   _____

      _____   _____

      _____   _____

     _____   Sales

      _____   _____

      _____   _____

      _____   _____

      _____   _____

      _____   _____

      _____   _____

      _____   _____

     _____   Marketing

      _____   _____

      _____   _____

      _____   _____

     _____   Human Resources

      _____   _____

      _____   _____

_____ We need to create or update our LinkedIn
company page and strategy

_____ We need to better develop, nurture, and expand
individual LinkedIn networks

    _____ Leadership   _____ Sales

    _____ Marketing   _____ Human Resources/
                                        Recruiting

_____ We need to better align our connections with our CRM

_____ We need to create or enhance our activity on LinkedIn

_____ We need to work with someone who can manage our online
presence for us

_____ We need to update our website

_____ We need to create original content (videos, blogs,
case studies, etc.)

Custom priority _____

_____

When will you start your most important action?

Date: _____   Completion Date: _____

What specific steps will you take to develop, launch, implement, review, and measure your corporate LinkedIn initiative?

1. _____

2. _____

3. _____

4. _____

5. _____

6. _____

7. _____

8. _____

9. _____

10. _____

What will you consider a successful LinkedIn initiative?

1. _____

2. _____

3. _____

Leveraging our **It's Business, Not Social™** methodology will ensure you have a proven process oriented to properly help you and your business **STANDOUT**.

A **STANDOUT** Commitment

A **STANDOUT** signifies someone who views their career and business initiatives with a long-term commitment and view.

Our definition of **STANDOUT**: **S**ignificance over **T**ime with **A**uthenticity, **N**etworking, **D**edication, **O**pen-mindedness, **U**nderstanding, and **T**enacity.

This should be everyone's number one career priority.

Seek opportunity with an open mind and curious nature.

Elevate your presence with purpose and clarity.

Approach your business and career with confidence.

Realize you are always in beta mode; learning and growing are ongoing and critical to business and career success.

Pursue opportunities with tenacity. Seek to expand your career with the highest level of authenticity and care.

Create context and showcase your experience, skills, talent, and community contributions.

Thrive by supporting and serving others.

Recognize that expanding a community of connections unleashes more business and career opportunities.

Become a Center of Influence.

Understand how to build communities, not just connections.

Always create an impression.

Believe that people want to do business with people who value you and your business.

Focus on quantifiable business and career results, not impressions, views, and likes.

Generate long-term social capital for yourself and your career.

Build your reputation by taking the time to develop strategic relationships.

Others will vet you online. Ensure you make a favorable impression.

Distinguish yourself by developing your skills, value proposition, and network.

Never compromise your value by accepting less than professional behavior.

Always identify, connect, and know the best talent in your industry.

Generate business by creating value in every conversation.

Press on even in difficult circumstances and economies by increasing your own marketability.